CW01373274

Wales

A Very Peculiar History

'In Wales it's eight different
weathers in a day.'
Actress Piper Perabo

First published in the UK in 2011
by The Salariya Book Company Ltd
This edition published in the UK in 2024
by Hatch Press, an imprint of Bonnier Books UK
4th Floor, Victoria House
Bloomsbury Square, London WC1B 4DA
Owned by Bonnier Books
Sveavägen 56, Stockholm, Sweden
www.bonnierbooks.co.uk

Copyright ©2024 by Hatch Press

1 3 5 7 9 10 8 6 4 2

All rights reserved

ISBN 978-1-83527-112-6

Printed in China

MIX
Paper | Supporting responsible forestry
FSC® C104723

WARNING: *The Publisher accepts no responsibility for the historical recipes in this book. They are included only for their historical interest and may not be suitable for modern use.*

Wales

A Very Peculiar History

Written by
Rupert Matthews

Hatch

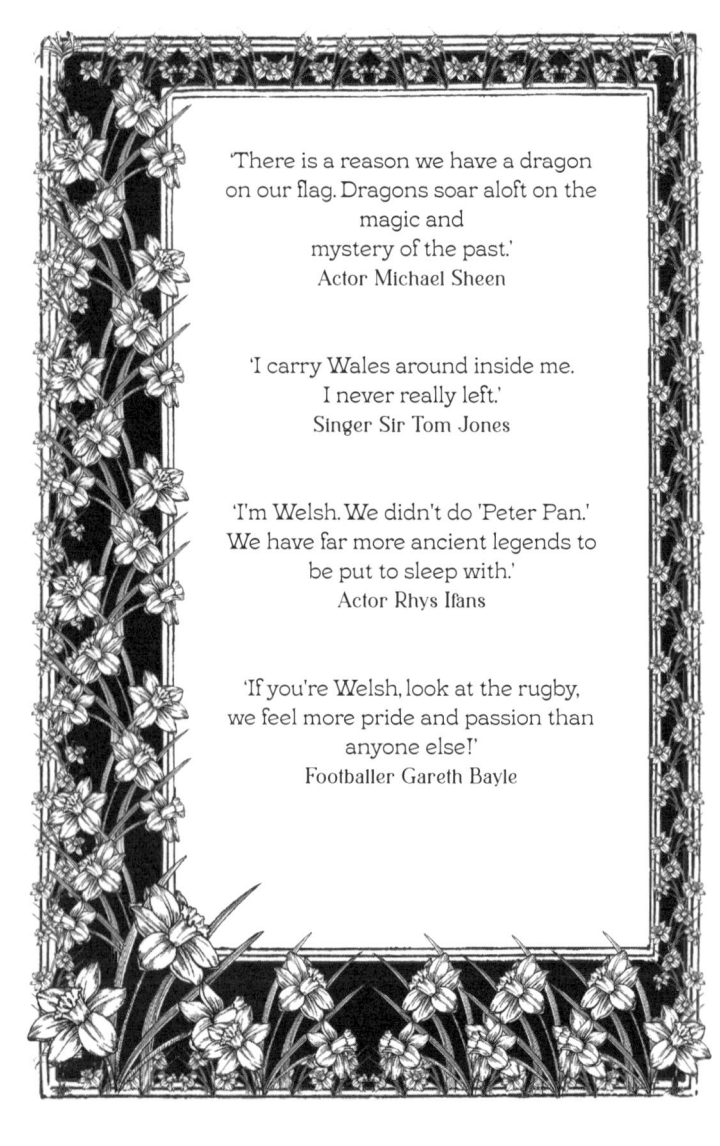

'There is a reason we have a dragon on our flag. Dragons soar aloft on the magic and
mystery of the past.'
Actor Michael Sheen

'I carry Wales around inside me.
I never really left.'
Singer Sir Tom Jones

'I'm Welsh. We didn't do 'Peter Pan.' We have far more ancient legends to be put to sleep with.'
Actor Rhys Ifans

'If you're Welsh, look at the rugby, we feel more pride and passion than anyone else!'
Footballer Gareth Bayle

Contents

Ten things to thank the Welsh for	6
Putting Wales on the map	8
Introduction: What makes Wales special?	11
1 The forgotten years	27
2 Resistance is Useless!	39
3 The Cymry Come Forward	53
4 The Princes of Wales	67
5 The English Wars	81
6 Castles and Cattle	101
7 England and Wales	115
8 King Coal	127
9 'Something Must Be Done'	147
10 Into the future	161
Pronouncing Welsh	180
Glossary	182
Timeline of Welsh history	184
Index	189

Ten things to thank the Welsh for

1. **Leeks** Welsh laws as far back as AD 900 impose penalties on any farmer not growing his leeks in a properly fenced field. Even earlier, around AD 250, the Welsh liked eating cooked leeks sprinkled with vinegar.

2. **Singing** Other people might warble a tune from time to time, but the Welsh can *really* sing. Go to a rugby match and listen.

3. **Suspension bridges** The world's first large suspension bridge was built in 1826 to carry the London–Holyhead Road over the Menai Strait between Anglesey and the mainland.

4. **The Pontypool front row** These three rugby heroes not only formed the front row for Pontypool, but also for Wales and the British Lions. In the 1970s, they won 15 out of 19 international matches. They were Graham Price, Bobby Windsor and Charlie Faulkner. Max Boyce wrote a song about them.

5. **Beer cans** A method of packaging beer into cans that did not affect the flavour of the precious liquid was pioneered by Felinfoel Brewery in Llanelli in 1935. Thirsty folk everywhere have been grateful ever since.

6. **Tongue-twister names** Welsh names can bamboozle English speakers. The village of Llanfairpwllgwyngyllgogerychwyrndrobwlllantysiliogogogoch on the Isle of Anglesey is more famous for its name than anything else.

7. **Tide power** Around 1550, a miller in Carew built a corn mill that was powered by a wheel turned by the tide flowing in and out of a narrow-necked pool. It operated for decades, but the idea did not catch on as most millers in Wales lived closer to a windy hill than a tidal pool.

8. **Accurate artillery** In 1776, at Bersham, near Wrexham, John Wilkinson invented a machine that could bore accurate holes in metal. It was used to make precision cannon able to fire shells more accurately than ever before. Not everybody has been grateful for this invention – especially if they were the ones being shot at!

9. **Airborne radar** In 1940, Edward Bowen of Swansea developed a radar set small enough to fit into an aircraft and powerful enough to detect other aircraft. Aircraft now no longer bump into each other at night.

10. **Slate Welsh** slate replaced thatch as a roofing material in the 18th century. The rats, mice and birds that used to infest the straw now had nowhere to live, and thus ended many diseases passed on by the creatures to humans.

1. **c.250,000 BC**: Oldest human remains in Wales are a tooth belonging to a person who died at Pontnewydd near St Asaph.
2. **c.3,500 BC**: The cromlech of Gwernvale is built to hold the tomb of an early farmer in the Usk Valley.
3. **c.250 BC**: Hillfort built at Llanymynech, covering a massive 57 hectares.
4. **AD 75**: The Romans build the great fortress of Chester, from which the II Legion Adiutrix patrols and controls northern Wales.
5. **c.450**: The fortress of Dinas Emrys is founded as a stronghold of the Princes of Gwynedd.
6. **1055**: Prince Gruffydd ap Llywelyn of Gwynedd captures and burns Hereford.
7. **1282**: Prince Llywelyn 'the Last' is killed at Builth, ending Welsh independence.
8. **1340**: The first recorded coal mine in Wales is in operation at Mostyn.
9. **1409**: Harlech Castle surrenders to Prince Henry, ending the last Welsh revolt against English rule.
10. **1780**: Bersham becomes the largest iron-working region in Europe.
11. **1804**: The world's first ever railway journey took place between Penydarren ironworks and Abercynon in South Wales.
12. **1819**: The Carmarthen Eisteddfod of Iolo Morganwg fixes the modern form of the festival.
13. **1966**: Carmarthen elects the first ever Member of Parliament from the Plaid Cymru political party.
14. **1999**: The first elected Welsh Assembly meets in Cardiff.

Putting Wales on the map

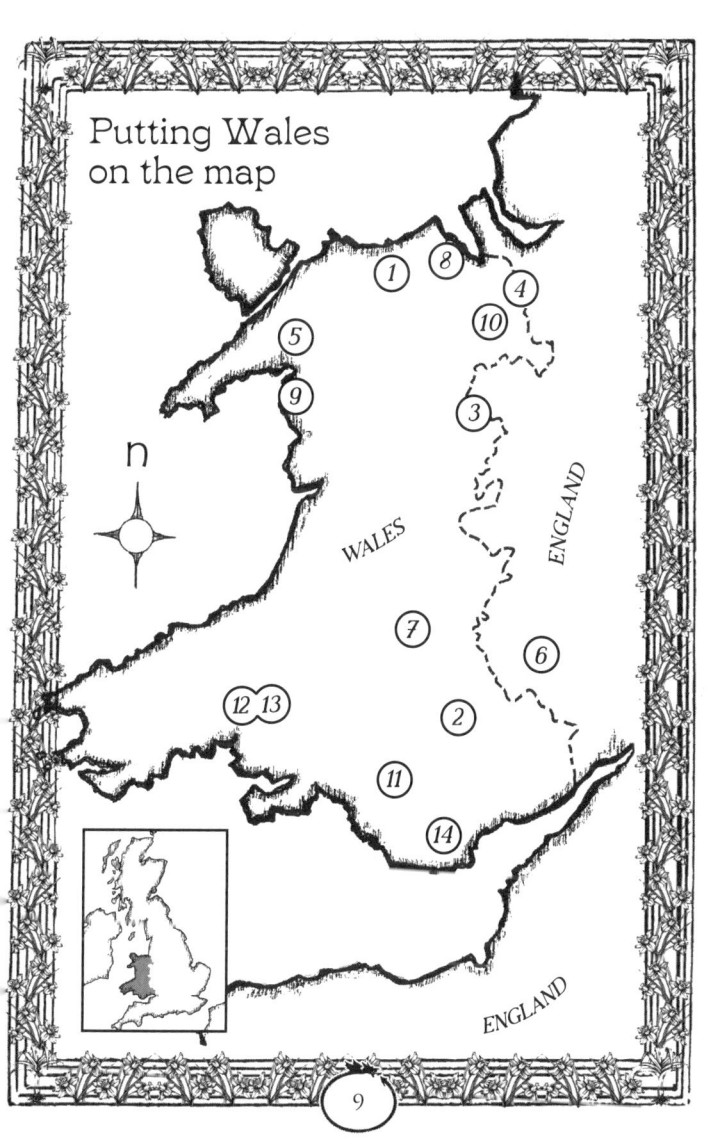

Some very peculiar facts

• The Welsh are a Celtic people. The Welsh language is closely related to other Celtic languages such as Scots and Irish Gaelic, Cornish, Manx and Breton.

• Although the Welsh were conquered by the Romans, they did not give up their language or culture. The Celtic peoples of what is now England were more thoroughly Romanised and no longer speak a Celtic language.

• When the Anglo-Saxons invaded Britain, they were unable to subdue the people in what has since become Wales.

• The border between England and Wales has varied over the centuries. Traditionally, the dividing line between the English and the Welsh was along Offa's Dyke (see page 65). It was considered a bit shameful for a Welsh person to be born to the east of the Dyke.

• The county of Monmouthshire was missed out of the Laws in Wales Act of 1542, which stated which areas were part of Wales and which were in England. Nobody was certain to which country it belonged until 1972, when it was made part of Wales.

• In 2007 there were calls for a vote in Monmouthshire to decide if it should be part of England or Wales. The idea was rejected.

Introduction
What makes Wales special?

Wales is a fantastically varied country. It has magnificent wild scenery, stunning coastal cliffs and wide, sweeping bays. It also has densely populated industrial towns, closely packed housing and, in places, great heaps of slag and mining waste.

The country occupies a rugged, mountainous peninsula jutting out from the western side of Great Britain, the largest of the British Isles. Several of the smaller islands off the coast are part of Wales. As we shall see, the character of the country and of the Welsh people has largely been determined by the scenic but harsh landscapes of Wales.

Wales A Very Peculiar History

Wales covers 20,779 square kilometres, stretching 274 kilometres from north to south and 97 from east to west. On the eastern side Wales is bordered by England, and relations have not always been friendly. There is even a great earthwork to keep the Welsh and English apart (see page 65)!

What's in a name?

'Wales' and 'Welsh' are both English words, and they are not really very polite. They are derived from the Anglo-Saxon word *walh*, meaning 'outsiders' or 'that bunch of softies over there'. At first the Welsh called themselves the *Brythoniaid*, a term embracing all those who spoke the Celtic language that later gave rise to Welsh and Cornish. However, around AD 600 they began to call themselves the *Cymry*, which means 'comrades' or simply 'us'. The two names were used alongside each other for a long time, but by around 1150 'Cymry' had taken over. It is the term most often used today by the Welsh.

Introduction

The sea laps at the other three sides of Wales, and the relationship with the sea has been just as important as the one with England. Long stretches of coastline have been designated as Heritage Coast by the government to preserve its natural splendour from development.

The north and central areas of Wales are mountainous, with 15 peaks rising to over 3,000 feet (914 metres) — they are known to climbers as 'The Welsh Three Thousands'. The south is best known for the Valleys, which run from north to south and have become heavily industrialised because of huge coal deposits. Here, the tightly packed terraced houses of close-knit communities are nestled into sweeping landscapes.

The climate of Wales is generally soft and gentle, though there have been some extremes. On 11 November 1929 the town of Rhondda received a massive 211 mm of rain in just 18 hours, while in 1962 Llwynon went through the whole of January with just 2 hours of sunshine. On the other hand, the Gower Peninsula is famous for its sunny summers and has a number of seaside resorts for holidaymakers.

Wales A Very Peculiar History

Most of the population of Wales is concentrated in the metropolitan areas of the south coast and in the Valleys, with the rest of the country having a more scattered rural population. The Welsh have their own language, descended from the pre-Roman Brythonic form of the Celtic language which was once spoken across most of southern Britain. Unique features of Welsh culture include *eisteddfodau*, a distinctive national costume, and a devotion to Nonconformist Christianity.

Leeks, anyone?

The night before the Battle of Hatfield Chase on 12 October 633, the army of Prince Cadwallon ap Cadfan of Gwynedd camped in a field of leeks. Next morning Cadwallon ordered each man to tie a leek to his helmet so that they could recognise each other easily in battle. The battle was a stunning success for Cadwallon. King Edwin of Northumbria and his son Osfrith were both killed and Northumbrian power was destroyed for a generation. The leek has been a symbol of the Welsh ever since.

The Welsh flag

The red dragon on a field of green and white did not become the flag of Wales until 1959. Before that date Wales did not have a formal flag at all. But the red dragon has been a symbol of the Welsh nation since at least the 700s. The colours green and white were those of the Welsh Tudor dynasty which ruled England from 1485 to 1603.

The design of today's flag was adapted from a heraldic badge which had been used on military uniforms since about 1490.

Visiting Wales

Hundreds of thousands of people visit Wales each year. Among the many reasons that they give for visiting are:

Outdoor sports

Diving: Wales is one of the best places in Europe for diving, with offshore wrecks, marine nature reserves and other underwater attractions.

Climbing: The Welsh mountains are among the craggiest in Britain and include some of the classic climbs of early mountaineering.

Caving: There are over a thousand caves open to potholers – mostly in the Brecon Beacons and the Gower Peninsula, but those in Eryri (Snowdonia) are just as spectacular.

Kitesurfing and windsurfing: The windy western coasts, combined with the warmer waters of the Irish Sea, are ideal for these popular water sports.

Canoeing: Welsh rivers offer a wide variety of whitewater and calm-water courses. The Dee, Usk and Wye are the best known.

Coasteering: The extreme sport combining scrambling, climbing, traversing, cliff jumping and swimming was first developed in Pembrokeshire in the 1990s.

The arts

Painting: Many people come to paint the wild landscapes of Wales. Others prefer to see what the masters of the past have achieved. There are many art museums, but the National Museum in Cardiff is a good place to start.

Theatre: The Millennium Centre in Cardiff offers free performances as well as top-end stagings of classics and new plays. Other theatres in the Principality range from The Met in Abertillery and Ammanford's Miners' Theatre to Newport's Riverside and the Wyeside Centre – offering something for everyone of whatever age.

Literature: Welsh writers are famous the world over. Visitors can see where they lived, experience the landscapes that inspired them and listen to their works being performed.

Music: Most of us associate Wales with male-voice choirs or touchline tenors, but Super Furry Animals, Stereophonics and the Manic Street Preachers are all from Wales, too.

Heritage

Scenic railways: There are old railways in Wales that run through the most fabulous scenery. Some were built to carry slate from quarry to port; others served remote villages in the days before cars. Some are narrow gauge, others standard gauge, but they all offer stunning views and a touch of steam-powered nostalgia.

Castles: Wales has the finest castles in the most stunning locations anywhere in Britain. They offer a masterclass in medieval warfare and construction.

Abbeys: The isolated valleys of Wales appealed to medieval monks, who constructed such wonders as Tintern Abbey, Neath Abbey and Talley Abbey.

Industry: The working history of Wales is on show at the Great Orme Copper Mines, the Welsh Slate Museum, Llechwedd Slate Caverns, Dolaucothi Gold Mine, Rhondda Heritage Park and many other locations.

National parks

Eryri National Park: There are 100 lakes, 90 mountain peaks, 60 kilometres of coastline and beaches, vast stretches of moors and wetlands – not to mention Yr Wyddfa (Mount Snowdon) itself.

Pembrokeshire Coast National Park: This park was designated in 1952 and covers about 620 square kilometres around the beautiful West Coast of Wales. It is the only National Park in Britain that consists mainly of coast.

Brecon Beacons National Park: The imposing sandstone bluffs that dominate the hills are over 470 million years old, but the main landscape features are valleys and lakes formed by the last ice age.

Food and drink

Quality modern foods: Salt Marsh Lamb is taking the smart restaurants of London by storm. Welsh black cattle are famous for the remarkable quality of their meat. Farmhouse cheeses and sea salt are Welsh specialities.

Farmers' markets: Held on a regular basis at over 40 locations throughout Wales.

Food festivals: Held annually, these include the Erddig Apple Festival, Llanerchaeron apple harvest display, Anglesey Oyster and Welsh Produce Festival, Caerphilly Big Cheese and the Real Ale Wobble at Llanwrtyd Wells.

♪ Gwlad, gwlad, pleidiol wyf i'm gwlad.* ♪

Traditional Welsh dress is based on late 18th-century peasant costume. It is rarely worn except on St David's Day.

* See page 137

'You've got to get your first tackle in early, even if it's late.'

Welsh rugby international (and bard) Ray Gravell fails to make his tactics clear.

Eisteddfodau

- Eisteddfodau (the plural of eisteddfod) are the leading artistic festivals in Wales. Some are small local events, others prestige affairs of international importance.

- Contests between poets, singers, writers and other artists are the main events at an eisteddfod.

- The first known eisteddfod took place in Cardigan in 1176. It was organised by Prince Rhys ap Gruffydd of Deheubarth.

- The word eisteddfod means 'a session' or 'a sitting'.

- The last of the great medieval eisteddfodau was held at Caerwys in 1568. After that there were fewer and fewer professional bards, so the festivals declined.

- The first modern eisteddfod was held in 1789 at Corwen and was organised by local man Thomas Jones.

- The most important modern eisteddfod is the National Eisteddfod, which lasts for 8 days in August. About 150,000 people attend, and up to 6,000 compete in the various contests.

- At most eisteddfodau, Welsh is the only language allowed to be used.

Wales A Very Peculiar History

Some famous Welsh recipes

Welsh rarebit
- 115 g hard cheese
- 3 tablespoons milk
- a little mustard
- a thick slice of toast

Grate the cheese and mix it with the milk and mustard. Spread the mixture over the toast, being careful to cover right to the edges. Grill until the mixture starts to bubble. Scoff while piping hot.

Cawl
The name comes from the cauldron in which this dish was traditionally cooked. Everyone in Wales has their favourite version – here's mine:
- 30 g butter
- 450 g neck of lamb
- 900 g leeks, thickly sliced
- 900 g potatoes, roughly chopped
- pinch of salt
- bunch of marjoram
- 2.25 l water

Brown off the lamb in the butter in a deep saucepan. Remove. Add the leeks and sweat gently until just becoming soft. Replace the lamb and add the potatoes, salt, marjoram and water. Bring to the boil, then reduce to a simmer and cook for an hour. Serve in bowls. Some people serve it with bread.

Introduction

Laverbread
Most Welsh people buy this in shops these days, but if you fancy having a go...
- 2.25 kg laver (a purplish seaweed that grows on the coasts of Wales and Ireland; collecting it from the tidal rocks is the tricky bit)
- 450 g oatmeal
- 225 g fatty bacon, chopped

Wash the laver thoroughly, then boil for about 5 hours or until it goes mushy. When cold, chop finely and mix with the oatmeal. Shape into oval cakes about 50 mm across. Gently fry the bacon so the fat runs out. Lift the bacon out of the pan and put to one side. Fry the cakes in the bacon fat until crisp. Serve with the bacon pieces.

Bara brith
The name of this dish means 'speckled bread'. When you cook it, you'll see why. Yummy!
- 225 g plain flour
- 1 level teaspoon baking powder
- 225 g demerara sugar
- 225 g dried mixed fruit (raisins and currants)
- 1 teaspoon cinnamon
- 1 egg, beaten
- milk as needed

Mix all the dry ingredients together, then beat in the egg. Add enough milk to reach a soft dropping consistency. Pour into a well-greased loaf tin. Bake at 160°C (140°C fan) for about an hour. When cold, slice and spread with butter.

Ten Welsh saints

1. St Dyfrig (or Dubricius) was born about AD 425 and died around 500. He was the last of the late Roman bishops.

2. St Illtud died around 550. He was abbot of the monastery at Llantwit Major and said to be the best-educated man in Britain.

3. St Samson was born about 486 and lived to be over 70 years old. In about 522 he left Wales to preach in Cornwall, and then in Brittany.

4. St Paul Aurelian was educated by St Illtud. Like Samson, he later moved to Brittany.

5. St Gildas was born about 516 and educated by Illtud. His book on the shortcomings of British kings is an important source for historians of the period.

6. St Leonorus founded several churches and monasteries. He once cleared a forest by calling up a storm to blow away the trees. He died in about 560.

7. St Brioc was born in Ceredigion about 520. He preached in Cornwall and established a monastery in Brittany. His ring is still kept at Saint-Brieuc Cathedral in Brittany.

8. St Teilo was Bishop of Llandeilo and went on pilgrimage to Jerusalem.

9. St Deiniol, Bishop of Bangor, died in 584.

10. St David is the patron saint of Wales.

St David

The patron saint of Wales is St David, or Dewi Sant. David was born the son of Sandde, son of King Ceredig of Ceredigion, himself son of the famous warrior Cunedda (see page 50).

David grew to adulthood around AD 540. The Romans had left Britain and the country was collapsing into near chaos. Much of Britain was overrun by the pagan English, trade with Europe had virtually ceased, and most Welsh farmers grew barely enough food to support themselves.

David believed the best thing to do was to seek the favour of God through prayer, devotion and plain living. He ordered monks to do heavy manual labour during the day and study scripture in the evenings. He never drank alcohol and was strictly vegetarian. He coined the phrase 'Comfort is the mother of vice.'

Many monks found David's demands for hard work and poverty too much to bear. They nicknamed David's followers 'the Betters'. Princes thought David's ideas about reading the Bible to defeat the English instead of fighting them were just plain silly. A lot of Welsh people found David deeply annoying — but others thought his ideas were wonderful and made him a saint. David died in 589.

You'd have got a chilly welcome in Wales before they discovered fire.

Chapter One

The Forgotten Years

Modern humans first arrived in Wales about 35,000 years ago, during a warm spell between two ice ages. No sooner had they settled in than another ice age arrived and forced the humans to move south to warmer parts of Europe. About 12,000 BC the icy weather began to warm again and people returned to Wales. This time they came to stay.

These first Welsh people hunted wild animals and gathered wild plant food. Favourite foods included woolly mammoth, giant deer and wild

Wales A Very Peculiar History

cattle. These big animals were relatively easy to hunt. The hunter-gatherers roamed around all of Britain looking for food. There were probably no more than a couple of thousand people in the whole of Wales.

Some time around 5500 BC the climate grew warmer and wetter, so that forests spread across Britain to replace the open grasslands. Living in Wales suddenly got a lot tougher. The big animals couldn't live in the forests, and they died out. People had to hunt the smaller forest animals and search for berries and roots to nibble on.

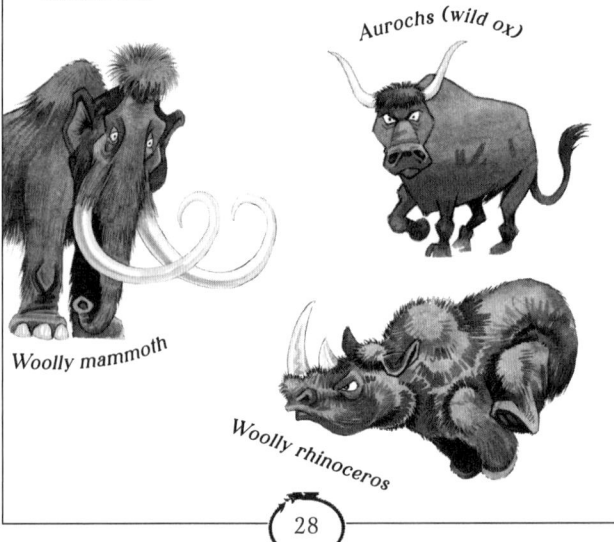

Aurochs (wild ox)

Woolly mammoth

Woolly rhinoceros

Settling down

This can't have been much fun, because about the year 4000 BC people in Wales gave up this way of life and became farmers. Nobody knows who the first farmers were. Were they immigrants from Europe who brought the new skill with them, or locals who learned how to farm by trading with the Europeans? Perhaps the introduction of farming involved both incomers and locals. Certainly the grains, crops and domestic animals raised by the first farmers came from Europe. These included barley, wheat, pigs, cattle and sheep.

Farming could feed far more people on a given area of land than hunting and gathering. The population of Wales increased rapidly and became more settled as farmers built permanent villages so they could be close to their growing crops. Forests were chopped down to clear more land for farming.

Now that people lived in one place instead of wandering about, they thought it worthwhile to make a mark on the landscape. They built tombs out of large boulders covered with soil; these are known today as *cromlechs*. Other boulders were set upright in circles or surrounded by circular ditches to form henges; religious rites may have been held in these.

The earliest farmers used tools made out of stone, wood and bone just as the hunter-gatherers had done. Then, around 2500 BC, a new technology began to be used: metal. At first copper was used to make tools, but soon tin from Cornwall was mixed with the copper to produce hard, long-lasting bronze.

About the year 2200 BC, beer arrived in Wales. An entire culture developed around the new drink. The 'Beaker culture' has been named after the distinctive bell-shaped mugs that are found in tombs. The Beaker folk used a wide variety of new metal tools, gold jewellery and weapons, and for the first time people wore clothes of woven woollen and linen cloth instead of animal skins.

Around 1400 BC the villages and farms began to be fortified with timber walls, earthen banks and ditches. Weapons became more common. This may have been because the climate was

The Forgotten Years

getting cooler and crop yields were falling. Perhaps there was not enough food to go round, and people had to fight for what there was.

Wales has more than 600 of these fortified places, or 'hillforts'. Of these, about 200 are small enough to have been home to a single family, while 22 could have held over a thousand people and were more like small towns. Many of the larger hillforts were built close to copper mines, gold mines or important trade routes. It seems likely that these were controlled by powerful chiefs who dominated large tracts of country.

Here come the Celts!

By about 500 BC or so, the Celtic culture had arrived. This doesn't necessarily mean that large numbers of people had moved into Wales from the Celtic heartlands on the continent. It's possible that the locals simply adopted Celtic customs, in much the same way as British teenagers adopted American culture by drinking cola, eating burgers and wearing baseball caps. The Celtic culture brought with it the secret of producing iron. Compared to bronze, this new metal made tools that were sharper and harder, but less springy and less colourful. The oldest iron object ever found in Britain was a sword, found at Llyn Fawr near Aberdare. Within a few generations iron would become much cheaper to manufacture. More and more tools and household items would be produced in this cheap, tough metal as Wales entered the Iron Age.

Celtic metalsmiths also produced some magnificent decorative items in a swirling, delicate style. All kinds of objects were decorated with gold and coloured stones. Many of the most beautiful items were deliberately thrown into bogs or lakes, probably as offerings to the Celtic gods. At Llyn Cerrig Bach on Anglesey the treasures thrown in included an entire war chariot, complete with all its fittings.

Driving the Llyn Cerrig Bach chariot could be a hair-raising experience.

Human sacrifice

At some Celtic festivals a criminal or a prisoner of war would be put into a large figure made of wicker and straw. The wicker figure was then set on fire and the victim burned to death. Other victims were beheaded and the severed heads were offered to the gods. The bodies were often put in pits or in bogs.

But sacrifices of animals were more common. The killing of humans may have been kept for special festivals or when a tribe or kingdom was in severe need.

Head hunters

After a battle, the Celts would slice off the heads of dead enemies and nail them up over the front door to impress visitors. If a warrior was very proud of the head of a famous enemy, it would be preserved in oil inside a chest. It would be brought out at dinner to be shown off to friends for the next hundred years or more. Each time the head came out, the family would tell the story of how it was taken.

"Another one for the collection!"

The Forgotten Years

The Celts of Wales eventually formed five major tribes. These were the Silures of the south-east, the Demetae of the south-west, the Ordovicii of the north-west, the Deceangli of the north-east and the Cornovii of central Wales. Each tribe was ruled by a powerful royal family, but there were many smaller noble families who were important locally.

Celtic warfare

For the Celts, going to war was an occasion for singing, drinking and generally strutting their stuff. Everyone wore their best jewellery and finest clothes while carrying weapons and armour decorated with gold and silver. The warriors formed up in dense masses while the nobles rode in front in their chariots.

Most battles began with the nobles dashing out in front of their armies to show off. They were skilled in galloping at high speed while juggling with their swords, doing handstands on the backs of the chariot ponies or dancing up and down the chariot poles. Nobles would dash forward to engage each other in single combat, with the armies cheering them on.

Wales A Very Peculiar History

Finally the main battle would start as the two armies charged forward. Celtic battles tended to be short, sharp and vicious. Very often an army that had seen its nobles lose in single combat would flee rather than fight. Winning respect was what counted, not numbers or fighting skill. In most battles, not many people were killed.

Once the battle was over, the winners would impose a penalty on the losers. This might involve handing over cattle, gold or other valuables. Hostages were often taken, and marriages might also be arranged as a way of making peace.

This method of waging war suited the Celts, who loved bragging and bravery. Men could work their way up through society if they were brave or lucky. But, although the Celts enjoyed a good fight, they were pretty much helpless when they came up against a ruthless enemy that was determined to conquer them.

And that is what happened in AD 47 when the Romans arrived.

Druids

The Celts' religious leaders were known as druids. These men not only organised the worship of the gods, but also acted as judges and gave advice on medical matters. They memorised the history and customs of their people and recited them in poems.

Most druids served a single tribe or kingdom throughout their lives, but some wandered from place to place. Druids from different areas may sometimes have met together, though what took place at these meetings is a mystery.

Boys began training to be druids at the age of about seven. They left their family to live with a druid, often in a sacred forest clearing or cave. It could take up to 20 years for the training to be completed. The trainee had to learn everything by heart, as the druids refused to write anything down – which is why no record of their teachings has survived.

Druids could intervene in any argument to bring about a final and peaceful settlement. They could even walk into the middle of a battle and order everyone to stop fighting, put down their weapons and start talking instead.

The Romans banned druids and chopped down their sacred groves. It is thought that druids continued to live in Ireland until around AD 650.

Welsh Gods*

Gofannan was a god of smiths and metalworking, but also cared for brewers.

Lludd had a hand made of silver. He seems to have been a patron god of royalty and rulers.

Gwydion was worshipped in North Wales. He was a warrior god and also a skilled poet.

Arianrhod was a goddess who cared for mothers, but not much is known about her.

Lleu was a warrior god who was especially skilful with the spear. He is usually called Lleu Llaw Gyffes – 'the Bright One with the Strong Hand'.

Manawydan was said to live at Gower in a hall built of human bones – which suggests that humans may have been sacrificed to him. He was a god of craftsmen.

Bran was a giant who was immensely strong. He had a cauldron that could restore dead warriors to life. He was also a skilled harpist.

Rhiannon was a beautiful goddess who brought fertility to the Earth. She was married to Pwyll.

Pwyll was the lord of the underworld, where humans went after they died.

See pages 180-181 for advice on how to pronounce Welsh names.

Chapter Two

Resistance is Useless!

Life in Roman Wales

In AD 43 the Roman emperor Claudius was feeling a bit fed up. Few people were taking him seriously as a ruler, because he stuttered, limped and was not as mad as his predecessor Caligula. He needed to do something dramatic, so he decided to conquer Britain. He did not lead the army himself, of course, but sent four legions and numerous auxiliaries under General Aulus Plautius to do the job for him.

The tribes of south-eastern Britain were either defeated or made peace with the Romans within a couple of years. But Caractacus (or Caradog) of the Catuvellauni tribe proved to be much more troublesome. After his own tribe was defeated, Caractacus moved west to act as a military advisor to the Silures in south-east Wales. The Romans followed, and in AD 49 they built a mighty fortress at what is now Gloucester. This would be a base for the XX (20th) Legion.

Caractacus and Claudius

For five years Caractacus fought against the Romans in Wales. Then he made the mistake of going north to the Pennines to talk to Queen Cartimandua of the Brigantes. She handed him over to the Romans. Caractacus and his family were taken to Rome and thrown at the feet of the Emperor Claudius. Instead of begging for mercy, Caractacus waved his hand at the vast city of Rome and asked Claudius: 'If you have all this, why did you want my wooden hut?' Claudius spared the life of the brave Celt and gave him property in Italy to live on. According to legend, Caractacus later became a Christian. His son, Linus, is said to have been the same Linus who became pope in about AD 68.

"Di immortales! Quam feroces sunt!"*

The Celts were not a soft touch for the Romans.

* Ye gods, they're a violent lot!

The top ten Roman forts in Wales

1. Isca (Caerleon): The largest Roman fortress in Wales, this was the home base of the II Legion Augusta from AD 75 to about 300.

2. Nidum (Neath) was built to guard a ford on the River Neath.

3. Maridunum (Carmarthen) was founded as a fort in AD 75, but by 130 had become a town.

4. Burrium (Usk) was built in AD 55 as a base for the XX Legion, but was abandoned in about 66 when the legion moved to Wroxeter.

5. Gobannium (Abergavenny) was built to guard the Usk Valley.

6. Kanovium (Caerhun) guarded a ford over the River Conwy.

7. Segontium (Caernarfon) was the largest fort in North Wales.

8. Bovium (Cardiff) was built for the army, but was later taken over by the navy.

9. Bremia (Llanio) was used for only 45 years.

10. Tomen y Mur (Gwynedd) has the finest ruins of any of the Roman forts in Wales, but the original Roman name has been lost.

Resistance is Useless!

Meanwhile, the new Roman commander, Ostorius Scapula, had marched to North Wales and persuaded the Deceangli to submit to Roman rule. He defeated the Ordovices in AD 51 and made some kind of agreement with the Silures. But the Silures were soon causing trouble again. In 52 they defeated the XX Legion, and then the Ordovices promptly rebelled as well. The legion then moved to Usk and later to Wroxeter — perhaps Gloucester had become too dangerous.

In 57 the new emperor Nero appointed a new commander in Britain, Gaius Suetonius Paulinus, and told him to conquer the entire island. Suetonius marched to Anglesey, massacred the druids gathered on that holy island and chopped down the sacred trees. But when Boudicca (Boadicea) began her rebellion in eastern Britain, the Roman invasion of Wales was called off.

It began again in 75 when the II Legion defeated the Silures and built a massive fortress at Caerleon. The Ordovices were crushed by 82. The Romans built roads across Wales, linking the 45 or so forts they had built.

Living the Roman dream

As far as the locals were concerned, the Roman Army was a great way to get rich. The army bought huge quantities of grain, meat and other produce from local farmers to feed the men. Even better, the soldiers were paid regularly and had cash to spend on entertainment, drink and souvenirs to send back home. One way or another, a lot of people in Wales made a good living out of the Roman Army. Each fort soon acquired a civilian village or *vicus* nearby – the one at Caerleon housed over 2,000 people.

The Romans wanted the local Celts to live in towns where they could be watched, taxed and controlled. In return, the Celts got Roman culture and had a chance of becoming real Roman citizens. They had their own town council, modelled on that of Rome itself, with elected officials in charge of roads, public entertainment, water supplies and so forth. Some civilised Celts even enjoyed Roman luxuries such as baths, amphitheatres and a forum (a public square where markets and meetings were held).

Resistance is Useless!

The most important type of town was the *civitas* (plural *civitates*), which was the capital of its own little territory within the empire. By about 120, Caerwent had become a civitas, and there was probably another at Carmarthen. These were wealthy towns surrounded by plenty of fertile farmland.

"Great, more gold for our masters...."

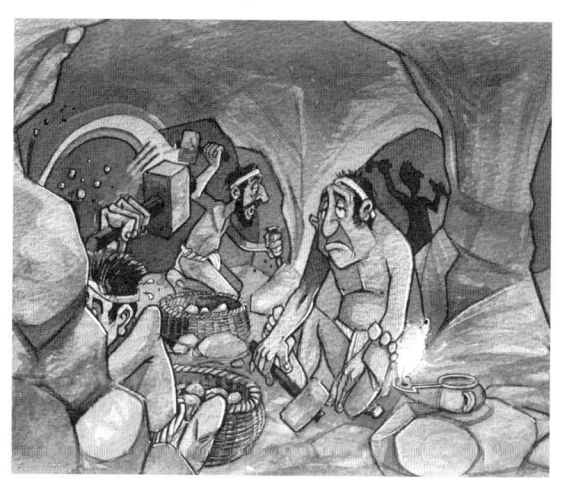

There's gold in them there hills! The Romans used slaves to mine gold at Dolaucothi from about AD 75 to about 350.

Them and us

Roman citizens enjoyed many advantages over the conquered natives. They could not be flogged, tortured or executed without a proper trial. They could vote and be elected to public office. They were exempt from some taxes and could own property free of local fees. Their children automatically became Roman citizens. Celts who helped the Roman state might be rewarded with citizenship. In 212 the Emperor Caracalla made all free men citizens of Rome. (Women and slaves didn't count.)

Dressed to chill

The Roman toga never really caught on in Wales. It was a loose garment that covered the body from the knees to the shoulders. It left the arms and legs open to the elements, so it was a bit draughty. People in windy Wales preferred to wear their traditional tunics, trousers and cloaks. The toga was worn only at very posh parties – or when appearing in a law court.

Goosey goosey gander

The Celts thought geese were sacred, but the Romans thought they were a tasty meal. Barnacle geese from upland lakes were their favourite. The birds were stuffed with a mixture of bread, eggs, pepper, chopped pig brain and peas, then slowly roasted.

A cash economy

The Celts did business by using barter and exchange. If a farmer wanted to buy a new ox, he would offer the ox's owner an amount of grain, a couple of sheep or some pots in exchange. This system worked well for the Celts.

The Romans preferred to use money, which allowed the Roman state to impose taxes and pay bills in an orderly way. A legionary, for instance, was paid 3 *sestertii* (large bronze coins) per day. Coins were a handy way of deciding what something was worth, and then paying for it. Coins could also be stored as a way of hoarding wealth.

Only the Roman state was allowed to mint coins, though they were produced at several different mints across the empire. The coins usually had a portrait of the emperor on one side. The other side often showed a god or goddess, but sometimes carried a picture celebrating a successful war, a new peace treaty or the appointment of an heir to the emperor.

After about AD 350, coins became rarer in Wales as Roman power became weaker. By 450, it was back to swapping sheep and grain again.

Wales A Very Peculiar History

The Celts farmed to survive, but the Romans farmed to make profits. They built themselves country houses, called villas. Each villa controlled a large area of farmland, growing crops that could be sold for cash. The Romans brought new crops that had never been grown in Wales before: oats, apples and root crops such as turnips, parsnips and carrots. Easily stored crops such as grain and root crops could be packed up and sold abroad — so could wine. The Romans did not rate wine from Wales very highly, though — they said it was thin and sour. (It's improved since then.)

Some of the villas could be both luxurious and large. The one near Llantwit Major had a bath house and family rooms with expensive mosaic floors. It covered an area of about 60 by 85 metres. The buildings were made of brick and stone and were roofed with tiles — very different from the thatched wooden houses of the Celts.

The hills and mountains of Wales were not ideal for farming, and were left pretty much as they had been in pre-Roman times. The local chiefs imposed Celtic laws, demanded tribute (a form of tax) and lived Celtic lives — though they

Resistance is Useless!

did have access to such prized Roman luxuries as wine and glassware. The chiefs were, of course, forbidden to fight wars, and the Romans probably made them give up the warrior bands that the old-style Celtic chieftains used to have. But otherwise they were left pretty much to themselves, so long as they paid their taxes on time and did not cause the Romans any trouble.

Even so, the mountain folk did benefit from Roman rule. The Romans brought new types of cattle from southern Europe, which were bigger and stronger than the native breeds. The large numbers of cattle and sheep raised in the hills were driven to be sold in the Roman towns where people were not only hungry for meat, but rich enough to afford it. Some British cattle even got as far as the Alps before they were eaten.

A Roman villa

Cunedda and his sons

Many Welsh legends talk about the warrior Cunedda, who came from the Votadini tribe of what is now southern Scotland to fight off the Irish invaders of northern Wales. Cunedda married Gwawl, daughter of Old King Cole of York, whom we all remember as being 'a merry old soul'. Cunedda had nine sons. Most of the noble families of Wales claimed descent from one or other of the sons.

The fatal road to Italy

In 383 Magnus Maximus, commander of Roman forces in Britain, murdered Emperor Gratian and grabbed power in Britain, Gaul, Spain and North Africa. But when he marched into Italy he was killed by Theodosius I, the ruler of the eastern part of the Roman Empire. Magnus Maximus is remembered in Welsh legend as the kindly ruler Macsen Wledig.

In 407 much the same thing happened again. Constantinus, the commander of Roman forces in Britain, declared himself Emperor Constantine III and seized control of Britain, Gaul and Spain. Entering Italy in 410, he was killed by men loyal to the rival emperor, Honorius. According to one Welsh legend, Constantine was grandfather to King Arthur, no less.

Resistance is Useless!

The dream goes sour

By 250 Britain was a prosperous and increasingly Romanised society. Then things began to go wrong. The economy of the Roman Empire started to fail, and there was a series of civil wars among the emperors in Rome. Then, seeing how weak the Romans had become, barbarians from outside the empire thought they would try their luck. It was too good an opportunity to miss.

Irish raiders came across the sea to attack coastal areas of Wales. Boatloads of warriors would come ashore to grab what they could, then escape back to sea if the locals put up a fight. As early as 260, some towns built stone walls to defend themselves. Around 320, a naval base was built in Cardiff, from which warships could patrol the western seas.

In 367 the Irish teamed up with the Picts from Scotland and with Germanic raiders from over the North Sea. They overwhelmed both army and navy to plunder across Britain. By the time these barbarians had been driven back, the economy of Roman Britain had been badly damaged. By 390, the market in farm produce had collapsed. Irish settlers were moving in to take over the rich farmlands of the Lleyn Peninsula and the far south-west.

In 410, the Romans who ran the British towns asked the Emperor Honorius to send army units to drive off the invaders. Honorius told them that he could spare neither men nor money to defend Britain. They would have to defend themselves. Most Romans assumed that things would get better, but they didn't. Roman rule over Britain had ended.

The first martyrs

On 1 July 304, two Christians named Aaron and Julius were executed at Caerleon. Their crime was that they refused to sacrifice to the Roman gods. The new religion of Christianity may have come to Britain as early as 150, but it took a long time to catch on. In 314 three British bishops travelled to a conference in Gaul (France), but the Welsh would not become fully Christianised for many years to come.

Chapter Three

The Cymry Come Forward

Wales after the Romans

The years after the Romans abandoned Britain in AD 410 are among the most obscure in Welsh history. What we do know is that in 410 Wales was part of a Roman province, but by 750 it was home to a new nation: the Cymry, or Welsh.

It would seem that the councils of the civitates (main towns) of Britain created a new position called the 'high ruler', who would organise the defence of Britain. This ruler, Vortigern,[1] followed standard Roman practice and hired

---

[1]. *Historians are not quite sure whether Vortigern was his name or his title; most believe that it was his name.*

mercenaries — soldiers who were willing to work for anyone who paid them. He chose two Saxon brothers, Hengist and Horsa, and their warband.

Big mistake! In about 440, a quarrel between Vortigern and Hengist led to warfare that devastated much of southern Britain. The peace treaty handed the civitas of Cantium (Kent) to Hengist, who set himself up as an independent ruler — or 'king' in his language. Soon other mercenaries did the same.

Princes in charge

In Roman times the local rulers in Wales were often given Roman-style titles and finery — partly to make them look more important to the locals, and partly to remind them who was really in charge. Some were given the title of *princeps*, which means 'first citizen' — or 'top man'. Later, the English form of this word — 'prince' — was used as the title for an independent ruler in Welsh areas. It was the equivalent of 'king' in English areas.

The red dragon rises

According to legend, Vortigern ordered a castle to be built on the River Glaslyn in Gwynedd. His men worked hard, but every night an earthquake struck and the building collapsed.

Vortigern sent for a boy named Ambrosius Aurelianus, who magically revealed that two dragons were fighting in a cave beneath the site of the castle: a red dragon of Britain and a White dragon of the invading Germanic mercenaries. Ambrosius foretold that the red dragon would win and rise up from the ground.

Vortigern then gave the fortress to Ambrosius – hence its name, Dinas Emrys, which means 'the stronghold of Ambrosius'. The red dragon became a symbol of Welsh resistance against the English.

Wales A Very Peculiar History

At first, the Romano-Britons — the British people who had learnt Roman ways — didn't feel threatened by these small Germanic kingdoms. Vortigern was more bothered by a local rival called Ambrosius Aurelianus, who may have been from somewhere near Eryri. Ambrosius probably took over as leader of the Romano-Britons some time around 470. He may have been followed by a shadowy figure called Uther, his younger brother. During these years the Germanic kings were gaining power, wealth and lands.

Almost as obscure as Uther was the man who is said to have been his son, and who succeeded him as leader of the Britons: Arthur.

"To Camelot!"

King Arthur: minor British chieftain, or legendary knight in shining armour?

Merlin was the wizard at King Arthur's court. Stories about him are based on the bard and prophet Myrddin Wyllt, who lived in Scotland's Tweed Valley around 580.

The Cymry Come Forward

Arthur

Historians don't agree as to whether Arthur ever really existed, or — if he did exist — what he did and how he did it. Arthur probably took office about the year 500. In about 516 he led the Britons to a great victory over the Saxons. This battle was at Badon Hill, which was certainly in southern Britain and may have been near Bath.

Despite this victory, things went from bad to worse. Disease, famine and poverty stalked the land. Tyrants and military hard men took over the government of the civitates. The bishops gave up preaching Christianity and acted more like greedy landowners.

According to legend, these various local troubles led to a civil war between Arthur and his nephew Mordred. Both leaders and most of their warriors were killed in the fighting, which left the way clear for the Germanic kings to surge forward. The time of the Anglo-Saxons had arrived.

Wales A Very Peculiar History

Whether this story is true or not, certainly something happened that caused British power to collapse around the year 550. The Angles and Saxons, those mercenaries from northern Germany and Denmark, muscled in. Within the space of just a few years, King Ida founded the kingdom of Bernicia, centred on the stronghold of Bamburgh in present-day Northumberland; Mercia was founded in what is now the Midlands; and other Anglo-Saxon rulers began enlarging their kingdoms.

In this time of uncertainty, when British rule had collapsed and Germanic power was growing, the British scholar Gildas wrote a famous book, *On the Ruin and Conquest of Britain*. In it he pleaded for the British to stand up to the invaders.

Nobody listened. Within a generation the Germanic invaders had utterly crushed the old Roman system of government and replaced it with a patchwork of small kingdoms. These people soon came to be known by a new name: the English.

Maelgwn the nasty Dragon

Maelgwn, Prince of Gwynedd, was known as the Dragon for his skill in war – but few people liked him much. In around 510 he grabbed power by murdering his uncle. He later murdered his wife and nephew so that he could marry the nephew's widow. He ruled Gwynedd from his fortress at Deganwy and surrounded himself with bards (poets) who sang songs about 'what a nice chap he was really.' He died during a plague in 547.

A lost opportunity

The British almost defeated the Germanic invaders in 593. Prince Urien, known as 'the Pillar of Britain', formed an alliance of rulers of what is now Wales and northern Britain. He led a joint army against the English. He crushed them in battle and drove them back to the fortress of Bamburgh.

But, just as he looked like winning the siege of Bamburgh, Urien was murdered by a man named Lovan – apparently paid by Morcant, who ruled the lands south of the River Forth. 'He was killed through jealousy, because his military skill and courage surpassed that of all other rulers,' said one writer of the time. Urien's alliance collapsed immediately.

They hadn't a prayer

The Battle of Chester in 616 was a major defeat of three Welsh princes by King Athelfrith of Northumbria. A procession of 1,200 monks came from Welsh monasteries to pray for victory. Athelfrith had the entire lot massacred.

The Cymry Come Forward

England and Wales

It was about this time that the Britons began to call themselves by a new name as well: the Cymry.[1] The word means 'comrades' or 'ourselves', and they probably chose it to contrast the Christian Britons with the pagan invaders.

In the wake of the sudden British collapse, the Cymry rallied around their princes. They held on to power in many areas that are now part of England or Scotland. As late as 650, Cornwall, Devon and much of Dorset and Somerset formed the independent state of Dumnonia. Most of Lancashire, Cumbria and Strathclyde were independent Cymric states.

In what was to become Wales, princes came and went, but gradually seven main areas formed. In the north-west, Gwynedd was the largest and most powerful state. In the south-west were Dyfed and Ceredigion, which later merged to form Deheubarth. Gwent, Brycheiniog and Glywysing were smaller states in the south-east.

1. Pronounced 'CUM-ree' or 'K'M-ree'. The Welsh name for Wales is Cymru, pronounced the same.

Wales A Very Peculiar History

The central area was covered by Powys, which had its capital at what is now Shrewsbury and stretched many miles to the east. Prince Eliseg of Powys, who ruled around 750, seems to have been the last Welsh prince to rule these fertile lands.

In about 770 the lowlands by the River Severn, which had been part of Powys, were captured for the English by King Offa of Mercia. Over the years that followed the English kings and Welsh princes continued to fight over this land, but the border between the two nations would rarely differ by more than a day's march from what it was in 770. England had become England and Wales had become Wales.

Within Wales, though everyone spoke the same language, there was no overall ruler. It would not be long before a man came forward who wanted to put that right.

Offa's Dyke

King Offa of Mercia built a vast defensive wall of earth to mark the border between his kingdom and the Welsh. Offa's Dyke runs for 240 kilometres from the sea at Prestatyn to the sea at Chepstow, with only short breaks where a river, swamp or dense forest formed a good enough boundary.

The route of the dyke veers off in places to ensure that a fortress, river crossing or other important feature lies on the Welsh side. It looks as though the English and the Welsh agreed between them where the border should be.

Offa did not station troops along the entire route. Instead, the dyke seems to have been designed to make travellers go through special gates where the English could keep an eye on them and, perhaps, make them pay taxes. The dyke stood almost three metres tall – perhaps higher, if it had a wooden fence along its top – and carts and cattle would not have been able to sneak across.

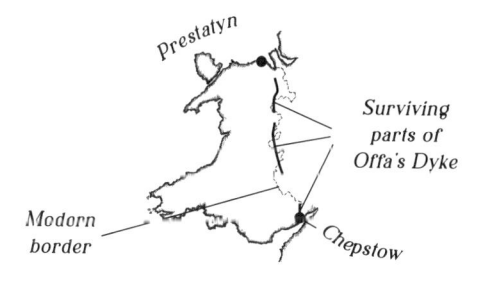

Prestatyn

Surviving parts of Offa's Dyke

Modern border

Chepstow

The Welsh language is born

The Welsh language, or Cymraeg, is descended from a language that scholars call 'P-Celtic'. This was spoken all across southern Britain before the Romans invaded. The language changed dramatically between about 500 and 600 to produce what we call Primitive Welsh. After the Battle of Chester the speakers of this language were divided between Wales, Cornwall, Cumbria and Strathclyde. The languages then developed in different directions, with a form of Welsh that could be understood by modern speakers emerging by around 1200.

Marwnad Cynddylan

In about 850 a monk wrote down a poem he had heard called 'Marwnad Cynddylan' – the Lament for Cynddylan. It was written in memory of Prince Cynddylan, who was killed by the English when they captured the Severn Valley. It is one of the oldest surviving poems in Welsh. It ends:

Gone are my brothers from the banks of the Severn...
Sad am I, my God, that I am yet alive....
Brothers I had who never lost heart,
Brothers who grew like hazel saplings.
All are gone, one by one, they are gone.

Chapter Four

The Princes of Wales

The Wales that emerged from this chaos after the fall of Roman Britain was almost the same size as today's Wales. The other parts of Roman Britain that were ruled by Celtic princes — Cornwall and Cumbria — were both taken over by England before 850.

At this date, Wales was made up of about a dozen small states, each ruled by a man who called himself 'prince'. These princes spent much of their time fighting wars against each other. Sometimes they tried to conquer the

Wales A Very Peculiar History

other prince and grab his lands; more often, the aim was to force the other prince to make regular payments of money or goods (known as 'tribute') and generally behave like an underling.

The constant squabbling was made worse by the fact that when a Welshman died, his wealth was divided between all his sons, and sometimes his daughters or grandchildren got some as well. Some princes divided their lands between their sons, creating new and smaller principalities.[1] Others would leave the title and powers of prince to one son, but divide up their wealth between all their sons. A prince was free to leave his title to any son, grandson, or even nephew, that he chose.

Think of the jealousy this must have caused! The son of a prince might be rich, powerful and popular, yet the title of prince might go to some cousin he could not stand. Murders, coups, rebellions and bloodshed among the royal families were inevitable. Between 950 and 1150 at least 28 princes were murdered, four were blinded, and others died in suspicious circumstances.

1. A principality is the land ruled by a prince.

Princely killings

The murderous feuds among the Welsh princes were legendary. For instance, in 983 Prince Arthfael ap Nowy of Gwent died and his place was taken by his two cousins, Rhodri ap Elisedd and Gruffydd ap Elisedd.* In 1015 these two were murdered by another cousin, Edwyn ap Gwriad. In 1045 Edwyn was blinded and flung into prison by Meurig ap Hywel, who was related by marriage to Rhodri ap Elisedd but had no real claim to the throne – except that he was tough enough to grab it. In 1055 Meurig was killed by Gruffydd, Prince of Gwynedd, who wanted Gwent for himself.

Welsh weddings

In the age of the princes, the Welsh viewed marriage as an agreement between two families, rather than a holy vow. Each wedding contract was different, with the bride and groom deciding who had rights over what, and what would happen to the children if the contract of marriage was brought to an end in divorce. Closely related people would marry if it helped to reunite ancestral lands.

Needless to say, the Church did not approve. Bishops tried to force couples to make permanent wedding vows but usually failed.

* *The Welsh word 'ap' means 'son of'.*

Wales A Very Peculiar History

There were several areas of rich farming land in Wales, separated by bleak mountains and hills. Each formed the core of a principality. However, no principality was large enough to lord it over all the others. And the English kings certainly didn't want to have a united Wales on their border. If any Welsh prince looked like getting to be too powerful, the English would step in to support a rival.

The Five Fertile valleys

Most of Wales is mountainous, or at least hilly. The soils are poor and unable to produce heavy crops, so in medieval times most families raised cattle or sheep to be sold in England, Ireland or other markets. Good farming land did exist in five fertile valleys: those of the Teifi, Tywi, Wye, Severn and Conwy. There were also comparatively flat areas of productive plains to be found on Anglesey, in the Lleyn Peninsula and north of Pembroke. These fertile farming regions provided wealth for several of the principalities.

The crops were usually raised by unfree families, ensuring that the wealth stayed with the prince.

The Five classes

In medieval Wales there were five classes of society recognised by the law:

1. the prince and his family.
2. the *bonheddwyr*, or people of known ancestry. They could own land and make legally binding contracts.
3. the *taeogion*, or unfree people, who were tied to the land that they rented.
4. the *caethion*, or slaves, with no rights at all.
5. the *alltud*, or foreigners, who had some rights.

In 700 around 10% of the population were *bonheddwyr*, but by 1300 that had increased to around 60%.

The history of Wales in medieval times was therefore one of almost constant warfare and violence — yet the nation itself remained both prosperous and highly cultured. This was largely because Welsh society was so stable.

In many areas, land belonged to an extended family group known as the *gwely*. Elsewhere there were villages known as *maerdref*, inhabited by unfree families who grew crops for the landowner. Each gwely and each owner of a maerdref was expected to pay a tribute to the prince who ruled them. This tribute — and the kudos that came with it — was what the princes fought over.

Fighting was generally the business of a small number of nobles and warriors. The prince rewarded his nobles with grants of maerdref villages, while the warriors were given jewellery and fine clothes, as well as food and drink. Each warrior hoped to earn the right to become a noble with a village or two to his name. This system encouraged almost constant warfare so that the warriors could prove their worth to the prince, and so gain richer rewards.

"Did somebody say 'rewards'?"

The Princes of Wales

Rhodri Mawr

Perhaps the first prince to become really successful under this pattern of warfare was Prince Rhodri ap Merfyn of Gwynedd, better known as Rhodri Mawr — Rhodri the Great.

By 878 he had united most of Wales under his rule and forced the other princes to accept him as their overlord. The English were worried that he would get too powerful, so in 878 they organised a murder plot that claimed the lives of Rhodri and his son Gwriad.

After Rhodri's death his lands were divided up by his three surviving sons. Anarawd took Gwynedd, Merfyn got Powys, and Cadell became ruler of Seisyllwg. However, now that Rhodri had created a ruling dynasty, it was here to stay — from this time on, all the main rulers in Wales were related to Rhodri.

Battles of Rhodri Mawr

Rhodri ap Merfyn inherited Gwynedd from his father in 844, Powys from his uncle in 855 and Seisyllwg from another uncle in 871. He ruled vast lands and commanded a great army, and soon won international fame as a warrior.

In 855 he marched over the mountains to Ceredigion, defeated the local prince and added Ceredigion to his realm. The princes of Dyfed, Buellt, Morgannwg and Brycheiniog accepted Rhodri as their ruler rather than risk a fight. In 856 he crushed a large army of Vikings that was camped on Anglesey under the command of Gorm.

But in 877 he lost a battle against the Vikings. The following year he was mysteriously killed – by Vikings, by the English, or by his own men?

The Book of Taliesin

This famous book, written out by hand about 1310, gathers together a host of poems that are supposed to have been written by or about Taliesin, a great poet of the 7th century. One of the most famous poems is the 'Armes Prydein' (Prophecy of Britain), which was composed about 950 and states that if the Welsh, Scots, Irish and Vikings could all join forces under a Welsh prince they would defeat the English. But what were the chances of that happening?

Anarawd meets Alfred

Anarawd was the son of Rhodri Mawr who inherited Gwynedd. He defeated a Viking attack on Anglesey and a Mercian attack on Conwy. Anarawd travelled to Wessex to meet King Alfred the Great, who was also facing the Vikings, to agree an alliance. Alfred gave Anarawd many gifts and some soldiers. Anarawd agreed to recognise Alfred as his overlord. Later English kings claimed that this agreement gave them the right to rule Wales!

"I'll be back!"

In 856 the Vikings were driven away from Anglesey by Rhodri Mawr, but for the next two centuries Viking raids remained a problem.

Wales A Very Peculiar History

Hywel the Good

In 904 Prince Llywarch ap Hyfaidd of Dyfed died without a son. His lands passed to his sister's husband, Hywel ap Cadell ap Rhodri, who was already Prince of Seisyllwg. The union of Dyfed and Seisyllwg created the new principality of Deheubarth. Hywel then conquered Brycheiniog and Buellt. Meanwhile, Hywel's cousin Idwal ap Anarawd of Gwynedd had taken over Powys. When he died in 942, Hywel marched his army north to seize his cousin's realm.

This gave Hywel even more lands than his grandfather Rhodri had owned. Unlike Rhodri, however, Hywel followed a policy of peace with England. He even went to England to pay homage (swear loyalty) to King Athelstan, accepting him as overlord.

Hywel concentrated on ruling his lands and collecting taxes and tributes. He also gave orders for the traditional laws of Wales to be gathered together into a single, agreed law book valid throughout all Wales.

The Laws of Hywel Dda

Prince Hywel ap Cadell of Ceredigion and Deheubarth was later nicknamed 'Dda', meaning 'the Good'. This was because he was responsible for having the laws of the Welsh written down and agreed for the first time.

Hywel travelled to Rome to see the Pope and study European culture. After his return he called a conference in 930 of nobles and scholars from all the Welsh principalities to meet at Hendy-gwyn (Whitland). He wanted them to agree on a single set of laws that would apply throughout Wales, ending the practice by which one place had different laws from another. The resulting Laws of Wales were written down and copies were sent all over Wales. Over the years some of the laws were changed, but they remained the basis of the legal system until English law took over.

Most of the Laws of Wales dealt with land ownership and inheritance – a very important subject in an agricultural society such as medieval Wales. Other sections covered relations between nobles, freemen, unfreemen and slaves. The gwely, or group of relatives, was very important in the Laws of Wales, as they decided matters such as land inheritance between themselves. The fine that had to be paid by a person who broke a law depended on his own status and that of the person he had wronged.

Wales A Very Peculiar History

After Hywel's death his sons divided up his realms between them. Much later, in 986, Hywel's grandson Maredudd ap Owain of Deheubarth decided to recreate the state ruled by Hywel Dda. He invaded Gwynedd in 986 and then conquered Powys, Buellt and Brycheiniog. After he had united his lands in 987, Maredudd spent much of his time fighting the Vikings. He was generally successful and on one occasion even forced them to pay him tribute.

Luckily for Maredudd, England was at this time ruled by the king known to history as Ethelred the Unready, who proved to be utterly incompetent at almost everything. He certainly failed to curb the power of Maredudd.

Unfortunately for Wales, Maredudd died without leaving any sons. He left his united realm to his son-in-law Llywelyn ap Seisyll, but Llywelyn had little wealth of his own. The nobles in each of the principalities that made up his realm chose their own rulers and the united Wales fell apart once again.

Oatcake rents

Rent for land was sometimes paid in oatcakes. Here is a recipe for oatcake rents.

- 900g oatmeal
- 2 teaspoons salt
- 4 tablespoons beef dripping, melted
- boiling water as needed

Mix the oatmeal and salt in a large bowl. Add the melted dripping and stir in enough boiling water to make a pliable dough that is not sticky. Knead well. Modern cooks prefer to roll the mixture out thinly and cut into 150 mm circles, scored into four triangles. However, the Laws of Hywel Dda state that to be used in rent a cooked oatcake has to be 'as wide across as from elbow to wrist and so thick as not to bend when holding it at the edge'. That's some oatcake!

The modern recipe should be baked at 180°C for 12 minutes, or until crispy and brown.

During the reign of Prince Llywelyn ap Seisyll of Gwynedd (1018-1023), raising cattle for export to England became the most profitable business in Wales.

Ten top Welsh monasteries

1. **Llantwit Major** was the first great monastery in Wales. It stood on fertile land close to the royal court of Glywysing
2. **Penally Abbey** is now a hotel.
3. **St David's**, founded by St David in 550, was the leading pilgrimage centre in Wales.
4. **Tywyn**, sacred to St Cadfan, was a major centre for religious studies.
5. **Penmon** was founded by the hermit St Seiriol, son of Prince Owain Danwyn of Rhos, c.580.
6. **Clynnog** was founded by St Beuno.
7. **Llanbadarn** was founded by St Padarn.
8. **Meifod** became the burial place for the princes of Powys.
9. **Glasbury** was founded by St Cynidr, who is buried in the church here.
10. **Bangor** was founded by St Deiniol about 620. It was endowed with rich estates by Prince Maelgwn the Dragon. Bangor Cathedral stands on the site today.

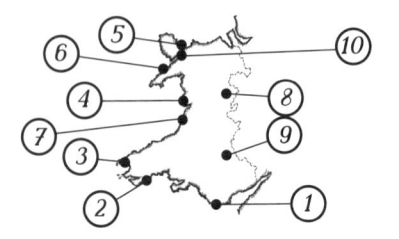

Chapter Five

The English Wars

There had always been border raids and occasional wars between Welsh princes and English kings, but things suddenly got a lot more serious in 1039. By that date the English were united into a single state, and Gruffydd ap Llywelyn ap Seisyll decided to do the same for the Welsh — with himself as the supreme prince, of course.

Gruffydd began by murdering Prince Iago of Gwynedd and grabbing power there, before leading an army to conquer Powys. In 1055 he had the Prince of Deheubarth killed and

Hereford Cathedral, 1055: not the best of times to be a monk.

The English Wars

marched in to seize control. The following year Prince Dawgan of Morgannwg heard he was next on the list, and fled. Other Welsh princes swiftly ran away or gave up their thrones, and by 1057 Gruffydd ruled all of Wales.

Gruffydd then teamed up with an English rebel, Alfgar of Mercia, and in 1055 they invaded England. Hereford went up in flames and Gruffydd took control of extensive border lands, killing or expelling the English inhabitants. Without doubt Gruffydd was the greatest Welsh prince ever seen. But it was too good to last.

England fights back

The English King Edward the Confessor wasn't going to stand for English farmers being pushed about by a Welsh prince, no matter how powerful he was. Edward sent the tough soldier Earl Harold of Wessex to teach Gruffydd a lesson and get back the border lands. Harold led a huge army into Wales and forced Gruffydd to flee into Eryri. There, the Welsh prince was killed by the son of Prince Iago, whom Gruffydd had murdered at the beginning of his career, more than 20 years earlier.

Edward was not interested in ruling Wales, so the English army marched home again. The various Welsh states chose princes from their own ruling families and the united Wales was a thing of the past.

The Normans arrive

In 1066 King Edward the Confessor died and Harold became King of England, only to be killed and replaced by the invading William of Normandy – William the Conqueror – later that year. The new Norman monarch gave the border lands to his toughest nobles and told them to get on with the job of keeping the Welsh under control. Any lands they managed to grab, he said, they could keep – so long as they did so as loyal English lords, not independent Welsh princes.

The border lands would become known as the Welsh Marches, and the barons who owned land there were called the 'marcher lords'. The word 'marches' comes from the Old English word *mearc*, meaning an edge or border. The French-speaking Norman lords made it their business

The English wars

"All we ever seem to do is march."

to take over as much Welsh land as they could. Some got land by legal means — marrying an heiress was a favoured tactic. Others simply launched an unprovoked invasion and grabbed as much as they wanted.

Bleddyn the Merciful

When Prince Bleddyn ap Cynfyn of Gwynedd was killed in war against Deheubarth in 1075, a monk at Strata Florida Abbey wrote that Bleddyn was 'the most lovable and the most merciful of all kings. He was civil to his relatives, generous to the poor, merciful to pilgrims and orphans and widows and a defender of the weak.' He added that the dead prince was 'the mildest and most clement of kings, who did injury to none, save when insulted'. He very soon became known as Bleddyn the Merciful – the only Welsh prince to be given such a title.

What a mistake to make

In 1090 Prince Iestyn ap Gwrgant of Morgannwg faced a rebellion by nobleman Einion ap Collwyn. Einion called in Prince Rhys ap Tewdwr of Deheubarth to back him up. Iestyn responded by calling for support from Robert Fitzhamon, Lord of Gloucester.

It proved to be a terrible mistake. Fitzhamon rode from Gloucester leading the legendary Twelve Knights of Glamorgan. He drove Rhys out and killed Einion. Then he turned on Iestyn. He threw him into prison and grabbed all his lands. Iestyn died a very quick and convenient death in Fitzhamon's prison a few months later – from 'natural causes', of course.

The English Wars

The Norman attacks began almost at once. They were helped by the fact that Wales had collapsed into a particularly savage series of local wars after the death of Gruffydd ap Llywelyn. By 1094 Morgannwg, Brycheiniog and Buellt had been overrun, while Powys and Deheubarth were crumbling as the Norman lords grabbed estates at swordpoint. Only Gwynedd held out, and even that state had to pay an annual tribute to England.

Then in 1094 a Welsh carter named Cynwric visited Chester, where he came upon a man chained up by the castle gate. The man was Gruffydd ap Cynan, a former prince of Gwynedd. Cynwric plied the guards with drugged beer, stole the keys and set Gruffydd free. Gruffydd hurried back to Gwynedd where he seized power.

In 1098, the marcher lords joined forces to invade Gwynedd, but Gruffydd called in allies from as far afield as Norway and crushed the invaders. By 1100 nobles across Wales had thrown off the agreements the Normans had forced on them and had driven the invaders out. Only Gwent, Brycheiniog and Morgannwg remained under Norman rule, though some Norman knights stayed on in Powys and Deheubarth, where they accepted the rule of the local princes.

In 1135 the Normans invaded again. Gruffydd ap Rhys of Deheubarth and Gruffydd ap Cynan of Gwynedd joined forces and defeated them at the Battle of Crug Mawr (or Cardigan) in 1136.

Norman tactics

The Norman lords were intent on grabbing lordships for themselves. This was their plan:

1. Find an excuse to invade – anything would do, even if it was untrue.
2. Build a castle.
3. Using the castle as a base, wipe out any Welsh lord with a warband.
4. Build a town and force the local farmers to sell their produce there, paying a tax to the Norman lord.
5. Finally, invent new taxes and impose them at swordpoint.

From Brycheiniog to Brecon

Brycheiniog was one of the smallest Welsh states. From 934 the princes of Brycheiniog were subjects of the English.

In 1025 Prince Bleddyn of Brycheiniog was attacked by the Norman baron Bernard de Neufmarché, who had married Nest of Powys and so inherited a claim to be Prince of Brycheiniog. Bleddyn died after being defeated in the Battle of Brecknock in 1093.

Bernard gave Bleddyn's son Gwrgan the estate of Blaen Llyfni on condition he would recognise Bernard as the new ruler. Bernard then declared himself to be lord of Brecon (the English form of the name Brycheiniog), and insisted that the area was now part of the kingdom of England.

The birds of Llangors

Just outside the village of Llangors, east of the town of Brecon, there is an island in a lake. An old legend says that the birds that roost in the trees on the island will sing loudly if the true ruler of Brecon visits, but will fall silent if a usurper comes.

When Bernard de Neufmarché grabbed power over Brycheiniog, he did not take the risk. He wisely stayed away and never visited the birds of Llangors.

Wales and the Church

After this, the history of Wales settled into a pattern. The Welsh princes paid little attention to the kings of England, but did their best not to annoy them. Welsh and English nobles and knights married into each other's families, and quarrelled and fought as usual.

At this time the Church in Wales was changing. So far, the monasteries had had more power and wealth than the bishops. Church rituals, priests' clothing and even some of their beliefs were uniquely Welsh. Officially the Church of Wales was subject to the Archbishop of Canterbury, but nobody took much notice of him. The Abbot of St David's was much more important.

But then a series of new popes cracked down. The power of the bishops was gradually increased. The old Welsh traditions were stamped out and new European-style rules brought in. The popes didn't think native Welshmen could be trusted to obey the new rules, so by 1150 most bishops in Wales were foreigners.

The Welsh discover America

According to legend the Welsh prince Madoc discovered America in 1170, three centuries before Christopher Columbus.

Madoc was a son of Prince Owain Gwynedd, and was sickened by the feuding among his brothers after Owain's death. He set off with a fleet of ships to try to find a new home over the western ocean. He came across a fertile land which may have been Florida, Kentucky or Alabama. He came back to Wales to recruit settlers, then set off again, never to return.

Madoc is described in medieval Welsh stories as a famous seaman, but the tale of his settling in America first appeared in the 1580s.

"Sounds a bit fishy to me."

Wales prospers

As the ability to read and write became more widespread among priests and nobles, there was an increased demand for books in Welsh and about Welsh subjects. It was at this period that many Welsh stories, such as those in the *Mabinogion* (see page 97), were first written down. Older documents that were crumbling away were copied out afresh, preserving much knowledge about earlier Welsh history and culture. This encouraged the feeling that the Welsh were a nation, not just a collection of small states.

At the same time, the population was growing quickly. By 1300 there would be more people living in Wales than ever before. These people were earning their livings in a number of different ways. As well as the traditional farmers and herders, there were now leather workers, weavers, goldsmiths and merchants. In 1100, Wales mostly produced raw materials to be made into goods in English workshops. By 1300, many of these goods were being made in Wales – and Welsh people were making a healthy profit from them.

"This should go down well in Abergavenny."

The Welsh know how to tell a good story.

The oldest book in Welsh is the Black Book of Carmarthen, a collection of poems copied by a monk in Carmarthen around 1250.

Getting a bad press

The English tried hard to persuade others that the Welsh were a disgraceful people. In 1159 Archbishop Theobald of Canterbury wrote to Pope Alexander III: 'The Welsh are Christian in name only, but really they are barbarians.' King Henry II of England was no more polite: 'The Welsh are a wild people who cannot be trusted,' he declared. Historian Giraldus Cambrensis, who was half-Norman and half-Welsh, wrote that 'The Welsh would be insuperable [unbeatable] if only they were inseparable [able to work together].'

The beautiful Gwenllian of Kidwelly

Born in 1097 as the daughter of Prince Gruffydd ap Cynan of Gwynedd, Gwenllian was said to be the most beautiful woman in Wales when she married Prince Gruffydd ap Rhys of Deheubarth in 1115. In 1146 the southern Welsh rose against the English and Gwenllian donned a suit of armour to lead the army of Deheubarth, since her husband was away. She attacked the English at Kidwelly, but was defeated and killed.

The field of Maes Gwenllian in Kidwelly marks the site of her defeat, and a spring of fresh water bubbles up on the spot where she died.

The English Wars

Llywelyn the Great and Llywelyn the Last

In 1194 Llywelyn ap Iorwerth became Prince of Gwynedd. Llywelyn wanted Wales to develop as a united kingdom with a single culture, a single law code, a single Church organisation and a single ruler — himself, of course. But he did not want to end up dead as Gruffydd ap Llywelyn had done. He saw that it was essential to make friends with the English, so he married the daughter of King John of England. He won the loyalty of the other Welsh princes and nobles. In return, he formed a Grand Council that advised him and had to approve his laws before they came into force. Llywelyn then swore loyalty to the King of England on behalf of all Wales. John recognised Llywelyn as Prince of Wales. He would become known as Llywelyn the Great.

Llywelyn the Great died in 1240 and was followed by his son Dafydd. By this time there was a new King of England, Henry III. Even though Henry was Dafydd's uncle, he announced that Dafydd was only Prince of Gwynedd, not of all Wales. Henry wanted the other Welsh princes and nobles to swear loyalty directly to the King of

England. War broke out and was still dragging on when Dafydd died in 1244. His nephews Owain and Llywelyn ap Gruffydd made peace with Henry III, accepting English rule.

In 1256, Llywelyn ap Gruffydd rose in rebellion and within two years had gained control of all the areas of Wales that were still in the hands of Welsh lords. In 1267 the Treaty of Montgomery was signed. This recognised Llywelyn as Prince of Wales, though much of southern Wales was excluded. Although Llywelyn could rule Wales as he liked, he agreed that the king of England was his overlord.

Despite this great success for Llywelyn, he had serious problems. His income as Prince of Wales was limited to traditional tributes, often in the form of cattle or grain. In the modern world of the 13th century this was not enough. Llywelyn tried to introduce new taxes, but unsurprisingly his subjects objected and he began to lose some of his popularity.

The *Mabinogion*

The *Mabinogion* is a collection of stories first written down in about 1100, though the oldest surviving copy dates from 1350, showcasing a rich tapestry of Welsh mythology and folklore.

There are three parts to the *Mabinogion*. First are the Four Branches, a series of linked tales that date back centuries, before they were first written down. Second are the Five Tales, stories about princes and warriors that may also be very old. Third come the Three Romances, stories about knights and ladies that were new in 1100.

Medieval bards (poets) were able to recite long stories from memory, so it is lucky for us that someone thought these tales worth writing down.

The Four Branches seem to contain many elements of pagan Welsh myths; certainly some of the characters are derived from Celtic gods and goddesses of pre-Christian times.

The Five Tales record early stories about King Arthur that are not watered down with later romantic inventions.

The Three Romances may be based on translations of French poems about King Arthur and his knights.

Wales A Very Peculiar History

In 1275 Llywelyn ap Gruffydd married Eleanor de Montfort. She was the daughter of Simon de Montfort, Earl of Leicester, and the niece of King Henry III of England. But the new King of England, Edward I, disapproved of the marriage. He sent ships to prevent Eleanor landing in Wales, and put her in prison. The quarrel led to war, which broke out in 1277.

Edward invaded Gwynedd with the largest army mustered in Britain for at least a century. Faced by overwhelming force, Llywelyn surrendered. Edward agreed to allow Llywelyn to keep the title Prince of Wales, but his lands were confined to Gwynedd and a few minor lordships.

In 1282, Welshmen in Hawarden rebelled against English rule. In June Llywelyn marched to support the rebels and captured several castles and towns. On 11 December, 1282, he was leading a patrol into Builth when it was ambushed by an English patrol and Llywelyn was killed. Llywelyn ap Gruffydd soon became known as Llywelyn the Last.

The adventures of Llywelyn's head

After he was killed, Llywelyn the Last's head was hacked off and sent to King Edward at Rhuddlan to prove he was dead. Edward paraded the head in front of his army, then sent it to London. In London the head was put in the pillory to be jeered at, then set on a spike over the gate to the Tower of London. It was still there in 1307 when Edward died. What happened to it next is not known for certain, but such heads were usually buried in the chapel of St Peter inside the Tower of London. Llywelyn's body, meanwhile, was buried in the abbey at Abbeycwmhir.

The noble Gelert

Just south of the village of Beddgelert is a small mound, the grave of Gelert the hound. Gelert was owned by Llywelyn the Great, who came home from hunting one day to find his son's cot overturned, the baby missing and Gelert with blood around his mouth. Assuming Gelert had killed the boy, Llywelyn killed him on the spot. Only then did he find his son safe and well beneath the overturned cot, together with a dead wolf. Gelert had killed the wolf to save the boy! Llywelyn buried the brave hound with great honour and, it is said, never smiled again.

The arms of Wales

The coat of arms of Wales is that used by Llywelyn the Great between 1199 and 1240. This consists of a shield split into alternate yellow and red quarters. Each red quarter has a yellow lion and each yellow quarter has a red lion. All the lions have blue tongues and claws and stand with one paw raised in the stance known as *passant*.

The current Prince of Wales has a personal banner for use when on official business in Wales, which shows these arms with a coronet (prince's crown) in the centre.

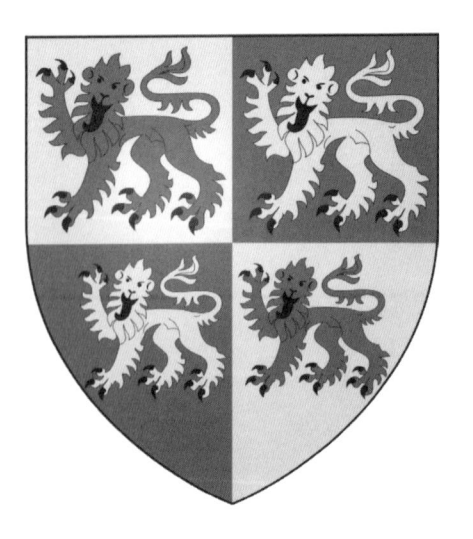

Chapter Six

Castles and Cattle

From Edward I to Henry VIII

The death of Llywelyn the Last handed Wales to King Edward I of England. There was nobody left who was strong enough to stand up to him. The Prince of Powys, Owain ap Gruffydd, chose to give up his title of prince and to take an oath of loyalty to Edward, just as the English lords did. In return he was allowed to keep his lands.

One of Edward's first acts after Llywelyn's death was to enact the Statute of Rhuddlan in 1284. This new law abolished the principality of Gwynedd and made it part of England. English criminal law now applied in Gwynedd as well, but for civil cases (arguments about contracts and inheritances, for example) the old Welsh laws of Hywel Dda remained in force.

The exiles

The heirs of Llywelyn the Last were sent into exile in England by King Edward I. His daughter Gwenllian lived at a convent in Lincolnshire. His niece Gwladus also lived in Lincolnshire until her death in 1336. His nephews Owain and Llywelyn were kept in Bristol until they died in 1325 and 1287. His brother Rhodri lived on estates in Surrey.

Rhodri's grandson Owain left England in 1356 to lead a company of Welsh mercenaries in the service of various European rulers. In 1372 he announced that he was the true Prince of Wales, and prepared to invade. The Spanish kingdom of Castile supported him, but he was murdered by an agent of the English government.

Castles and Cattle

Edward's castles

Edward then began the construction of a ring of castles around Gwynedd, to keep the country under control. Each castle was positioned so that it commanded a key road or river, and so that supplies could be brought by sea or by land. These English castles were hated by the local lords at the time, but are now popular tourist attractions.

Edward soon realised that the taxation and legal systems of Wales relied upon there being a prince. He decided that it would be best to appoint a new Prince of Wales. According to legend, the Welsh nobles got to hear about this and told Edward that they wanted a prince who had been born in Wales and spoke not a word of English. Edward thought about this for a while, then chose his baby son Edward, who had been born in Caernarfon and was not yet old enough to speak any language at all. It's a good story, and typical of Edward I's character. But unfortunately it's too good to be true: the young prince was actually 15 at the time.

Ten top marcher castles

1. **Abergavenny** is where William de Braose murdered Prince Seisyll ap Dyfnwal at Christmas dinner in 1175.
2. **Brecon** uses stones from a Roman fortress.
3. **Cardiff** was inhabited from 1081 to 1947, when it was sold to Cardiff Council.
4. **Carew** hosted the 'Greatest Party in Wales' when 600 nobles celebrated the knighthood of Rhys ap Thomas in 1507.
5. **Carreg Cennen** stands atop a 90-metre cliff.
6. **Chepstow** is the oldest marcher castle. It was begun in 1067 by William FitzOsbern.
7. **Coity** belonged to Norman knight Payn de Turberville, who got it by marrying the daughter of the local chieftain.
8. **White Castle** at Llantilio is one of the finest ruins of a non-royal castle in Wales.
9. **Powis** was begun in 1109, rebuilt as a luxury home in 1587, and is still inhabited.
10. **Pembroke** (opposite) was the most powerful private castle in Wales. It was captured only by starvation, never by assault.

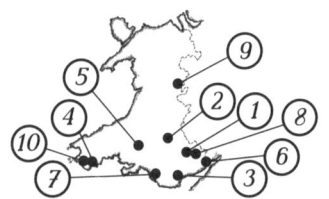

Middle Welsh

In 1283 Welsh was the language spoken by the vast majority of people living in Wales. There were just a few small areas of southern Wales where immigrants speaking English, Flemish or other languages were in the majority.

The form of Welsh used at this time is today called Middle Welsh. It can be understood, with a bit of effort, by modern Welsh speakers. Nearly all medieval Welsh manuscripts are written in this form. The English conquest made little difference to the language or how widely it was spoken – at least at first.

Ten new towns

Edward I was keen to found new towns and expand old ones. Some of them have done very well for themselves.

1. **Aberystwyth** now has a population of 14,600 plus 8,000 students at the university.

2. **Harlech** today has a population of 1,300. It is famous for the patriotic song 'Men of Harlech', a version of which is sung in the film *Zulu*.

3. **Criccieth** is now a rather quiet seaside resort with a population of less than 2,000.

4. **Caernarfon** has a population of 10,000 and is the capital of the region of Gwynedd.

5. **Newborough** was founded to hold the Welsh people Edward I evicted from other areas. It now has a population of 1,000.

6. **Beaumaris** was to be the main port of North Wales. It now has a population of 1,100.

7. **Conwy** still has its original town walls and has grown to a population of 15,000.

8. **Rhuddlan** was home to Gruffydd ap Llywelyn. Its modern population is 3,800.

9. **Caerwys** had a market before Edward I's time. It now has a population of 1,000.

10. **Flint** commands the River Dee and has a population of 13,000.

Castles and Cattle

In 1294 a rebellion broke out, led by Madog ap Llywelyn, a junior relative of the princely house of Gwynedd. The uprising was not well organised and was defeated within a year. Madog was put in prison in London, but spared execution. A rebellion against Edward II in 1315, led by Llywelyn Bren, also failed.

Wales under Edward III

In 1327 a new king, Edward III, came to the English throne. He appointed native Welshmen to various posts within the government and law systems. He also valued the fighting qualities of his Welsh subejcts, and recruited large numbers of them to fight in France. They helped him win his great victories at Crécy (1346) and Poitiers (1356), two of the most important battles in the Hundred Years' War.

This not only ensured a steady flow of cash into Wales, but also provided employment for large numbers of young men who might otherwise have caused trouble. Other young men left Wales to take employment as seasonal farm workers in England.

Meanwhile, Welsh society was changing. The old gwely system, where land was held jointly by members of an extended family, was breaking down as men preferred to own their own land. Gradually business contracts, land ownership and relationships between individuals became more important than family ties. The Laws of Hywel Dda, which were based on the family, fell into disuse.

In the towns, industries such as the manufacture of woollen cloth were becoming important. After about 1420, these trades boomed, bringing wealth and prosperity to Wales. Some of the men who owned town-based businesses became very rich indeed.

In the countryside, life was more traditional. Wealthy landowners showed off their new status by giving money and encouragement to poets, just as the princes had once employed bards. It was at this period that Dafydd ap Gwilym, perhaps the greatest Welsh poet of all time, wrote his passionate works about love and nature. Many people looked back longingly to the good old days as they saw society changing around them.

"Do you think the hat's a bit over the top?"

Welsh wealth

In 1390 John Owen of Carmarthon was one-tenth as rich as the King of England.

The drovers

After about 1300 the towns and cities of England grew rapidly in size and prosperity. This prompted the growth of the droving trade, in which Welsh cattle were driven over the border and on to the distant towns. Drove roads were often wide, and went over the uplands where there was grazing and few ploughed fields. Successful drovers became highly respected businessmen, bringing wealth to previously poor parts of Wales. The drovers and their roads remained a feature of Welsh trade and society until the spread of the railways in the 19th century.

The Black Death

The greatest disaster to strike Wales and Europe in the Middle Ages was the Black Death, a horrific plague from Asia that killed over one third of the population. The disease arrived at Carmarthen in March 1349 and at Abergavenny a few days later. Within a year it had swept across Wales, affecting every village and town. It is thought that about a quarter of the population died. Rents for the lordship of Abergavenny fell by 65% in just one year, while the law courts were closed for fear that the disease would spread in them. The uplands suffered less than the lowlands, perhaps because more people lived alone there.

Castles and Cattle

A new champion

One of the richest of these country landowners was Owain Glyndŵr of Sycharth, who was distantly related to the princely families of Gwynedd and Powys.

In 1399 King Richard II of England was overthrown by Henry IV. One of the new king's supporters was Lord Grey of Ruthin. Knowing the king was on his side, Grey seized some lands which belonged in part to Owain Glyndŵr. When Glyndŵr objected, Grey accused him of supporting Richard II and charged him with treason. Glyndŵr responded by calling out his armed followers, who declared him to be Prince of Wales.

At first the uprising was small, but by June 1401 Glyndŵr had control over much of Wales. In 1403 the powerful Percy family of northern England rebelled against Henry IV and sided with Glyndŵr. The Percy rebellion was crushed at the Battle of Shrewsbury, but many were convinced that Glyndŵr could win. Welshmen flocked to join his army.

Wales A Very Peculiar History

In 1404 Glyndŵr called a parliament of Wales and appointed a government. In the same year the English gained a new commander in the form of Prince Henry (later King Henry V). He quickly decided that he could not defeat Glyndŵr in the Welsh hills. Instead he began a strict blockade of Welsh ports, crippling trade and raising the spectre of famine.

In 1407 Glyndŵr's supporters started to desert him, and by 1410 Henry had effective control over most of Wales. In 1412 Glyndŵr vanished into the mountains. Although Henry offered huge rewards, Glyndŵr was never betrayed and his eventual fate remains a mystery.

Henry introduced the 'Penal Code', a new set of laws which banned Welshmen from holding certain government posts. The Code was not relaxed until the 1460s. Some posts were held by Englishmen who took the money but rarely turned up to do any work. And so the system of government in Wales started to fall apart, just as trade was booming.

Castles and Cattle

Red vs. White

'The Wars of the Roses' is the modern name for a series of civil wars between two powerful English families: the House of Lancaster, whose emblem was the red rose, and the House of York, who chose the white rose. Both sides owned land in Wales, and many Welsh noblemen fought and died on each side.

In 1485 a Welsh nobleman and Lancastrian supporter named Henry Tudor took advantage of his royal ancestry to claim the English throne. He landed at Milford Haven in South Wales with a force of French mercenaries, raised Welsh troops and marched into England to defeat and kill King Richard III at Bosworth.

Henry Tudor — now King Henry VII — set about reforming the government of Wales. He abolished the remaining powers of the marcher lords and replaced them with officials appointed by the king. His son, Henry VIII, went further. He passed the Laws in Wales Acts between 1535 and 1542. They are better known as the Acts of Union.

The six unlucky princes

Since it became traditional to grant the title Prince of Wales to the eldest son of the English monarch, six Princes of Wales have failed to become King of England:

1. **Edward the Black Prince**, son of Edward III, died of dysentery while invading France in 1376.

2. **Edward of Westminster**, son of Henry VI, was killed in battle 1471.

3. **Edward of Middleham**, son of Richard III, died suddenly in 1484, at the age of 11.

4. **Prince Arthur**, eldest son of Henry VII, died in 1502 of a mysterious disease known as the 'English sweat'.

5. **Prince Henry**, eldest son of James I, died of typhoid fever in 1612.

6. **Prince Frederick**, eldest son of George II, died in 1751 after being hit by a cricket ball.

Taking a long shot

In 1461, during the Wars of the Roses, a Yorkist archer named Llywelyn of Nannau was part of the garrison of Conwy Castle. A Lancastrian patrol appeared and began studying the defences. Llywelyn used his longbow to shoot dead a Lancastrian scout standing 676 yards (618 metres) away – the greatest range at which a person has ever been killed by an arrow.

Chapter Seven

England and Wales

From Henry VIII to the Industrial Revolution

Born half-Welsh and half-English, Henry VIII decided that the two parts of his realm should be brought together. He gave the job to his chief minister, Thomas Cromwell. Being English, Cromwell thought the English way of doing things was best. Between 1535 and 1542 he revolutionised the government of Wales, and in the longer term he had a massive impact on Welsh society and culture.

In law, the Welsh and the English became one nation, usually referred to as 'England and

Wales A Very Peculiar History

Wales'. Although the border between Wales and England was defined for the first time, any differences between the two countries were abolished.

The laws that enabled marcher lords and other powerful men to maintain private armies were scrapped, bringing peace and order to the countryside for the first time in centuries. The law courts were reformed along English lines: local nobles lost their right to pass judgment, and justices of the peace (local law officers) were appointed by the king. For the first time Welsh counties and towns could elect men to serve in the English parliament. Welsh was relegated to a second language, and Welsh marriage customs were replaced by the English system of permanent marriage vows – though for a long time many Welsh couples refused to abide by the new laws.

The well-off middle classes welcomed these changes, but the nobles and the poorer rural farmers did not. Many people today see the Laws in Wales Acts as an attempt to destroy everything that was different in Welsh culture.

"Well, that should sort them out!"

Henry VIII,
King of England
and Wales

Speak English — or else!

The 1535 Laws in Wales Act made it illegal to use Welsh in any official capacity anywhere in Wales or England. Welsh could not be used in law courts, legal contracts, government records, official correspondence or oaths. No government official was allowed to use Welsh when on duty, on pain of being sacked on the spot.

The Statute was repealed in 1887, but it was not until 1993 that Welsh was raised to the status of an official language alongside English.

Three rich squires

• The Bulkeley Family of Caernarfonshire were rich by 1450. By 1550 they controlled the borough of Beaumaris and chose its MP. In 1644 they gained the title of Viscount Bulkeley, but this died out in 1822.

• The Perrot family of Pembrokeshire were landowners in 1130 and by 1450 were the richest family in Wales. They always refused a noble title.

• The Wynns of Gwydir were descended from the royal family of Gwynedd. They gave their wealth to charity, founding a hospital and at least one school.

Printing Parry's Bible

England and Wales

Welsh learning

As these changes took hold, William Morgan translated the Bible into Welsh in 1588. The book contained a number of errors and was later replaced by Bishop Richard Parry's Bible of 1620, still the standard version. The two translations showed not only that Welsh was a language capable of written artistry, but also that there was a market for books in Welsh. Publishers took note and soon began to print various works in the language.

Meanwhile, the wealth of Welsh gentry and landowners was growing. Though they now had to speak English to do business and get on in the world, they continued to use Welsh at home and were proud of their ancient Welsh pedigree.

The bards of old faded away as the princes and lords who had employed them vanished. They were replaced by writers, poets and artists who relied on selling books for their income. The last bard employed full time by one family was John Davies, in the household of the Nanneys of Nannau, who died in 1694.

Alongside the new arts was a renewed interest in Welsh history. Robert Vaughan of Hengwrt spent many years collecting ancient manuscripts and studying them for historical nuggets. Others followed his lead.

The economy was booming as Welsh cattle, Welsh leather, Welsh sheep and Welsh wool came into great demand in England and abroad. Other crops were grown for local markets, but it was livestock that brought in the export profits.

The Welsh harp from Italy

In the 17th century large numbers of Welshmen earned a living in England playing the harp at weddings, dances and parties. By about 1650 nearly all of them were using a type of harp that had a triple row of strings, unlike the Irish and English versions, which had only one row. (The middle row of strings allows a full range of sharps and flats to be played.) The instrument became known as the Welsh harp, and is still made in Wales. However, the design had been invented by an Italian in around 1600 and brought to Wales by Frenchman Jean le Fielle in 1629.

Leeks and daffodils

After about 1600 the daffodil began to be used as a symbol of Wales. The Welsh for 'leek' is *cenhinen* and the term for 'daffodil' is *cenhinen Pedr*, which means 'St Peter's leek'. It is thought that the similarity of names caused the daffodil to be used by people who did not fancy pinning a large, smelly leek onto their clothes.

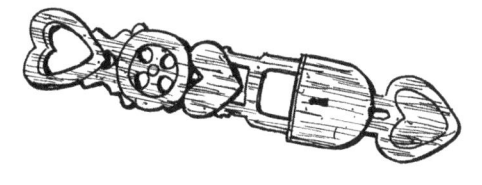

A romantic tradition

From about 1600 onwards, young Welshmen got into the habit of carving ornate wooden spoons for their girlfriends. The designs came to acquire symbolic meaning: a heart meant love, a bell indicated marriage, a horseshoe was for luck and a lock indicated security. The more work that went into the spoon, the more devoted the young man was supposed to be. In the 21st century, love spoons are given as wedding presents, anniversary presents or just for luck.

Siege of Harlech Castle, 1647

England and Wales

The Civil War and after

In the English civil wars of the mid-17th century, the Welsh overwhelmingly backed King Charles I against Parliament. But Charles lost, and many Welsh families lost their wealth as he lost his head. Harlech Castle was the last fortress in Britain to hold out for Charles; it finally surrendered on 16 March 1647, long after Charles himself had been captured.

After the victory of Parliament, the new government dismissed 278 clergymen in Wales who were thought to be royalists. They were replaced by others, often wandering preachers of unorthodox faith. Although most Welsh people still belonged to the official Church, many were attracted to the smaller Protestant churches which are referred to as 'Nonconformist'.

After about 1740, the most important Nonconformist group was the Methodists, led by John Wesley of Lincolnshire. In Wales the Methodist Revival saw a great upsurge in religious devotion, charitable works and education. This new form of Christianity remained officially within the Church for the time being. The idea of splitting the established Church did not appeal — yet.

Restoration Wales

In August 1659 landowner Thomas Myddelton stood up in a street in Wrexham and declared the exiled Charles II to be King of England and Wales. He was cheered by the crowd, but the army soon cleared the streets. Ten months later Myddelton did it again, but now his timing was much better. The army had switched sides and naval ships were bringing home the exiled monarch.

The decades that followed the restoration of Charles II saw changes in Welsh society. There were fewer landowners, as families increased the size of their estates by marrying into other landowning families. As a few men became wealthier and more important, their grip on power increased. By 1714 only 10% of Welsh members of parliament were elected. All the others were chosen by behind-closed-doors deals among the local gentry.

Three great Methodists

• Daniel Rowland (1713-1790) was a curate at Llangeitho when he began preaching about the judgement of God on sinful humanity. He founded his own chapel and congregation.

• William Williams 'Pantycelyn' (1717-1791) was a powerful preacher, but is better known for his magnificent hymns. They were published in a book with the not very exciting title of *Ychydig Hymnau* ('A Few Hymns').

• Howell Harris (1714-1773) walked across Wales preaching God's forgiveness. His funeral attracted over 20,000 mourners.

The circulating schools

Traditionally there were few schools and only the sons of the gentry and the rich attended them. Then, in 1731, Griffith Jones, vicar of Llanddowror, founded a novel type of school. It taught in a village for three months, teaching the locals reading, writing, arithmetic and basic religious knowledge. Lessons were in Welsh. The school then moved on to another village to educate a fresh intake of pupils. In the course of a few years it would circulate around a district. Soon other circulating schools were founded, and within 30 years over 200,000 people had attended.

The Industrial Revolution approaches

Meanwhile, industry was once again on the increase, though its spread was as yet rather patchy. First Neath and then Swansea grew as copper-smelting towns, and by 1750 they were between them producing 50% of all British copper. Iron was also a growing business, with smelting works being established at Pontypool, Bersham and Merthyr Tydfil in the first half of the 18th century. Coalmining was on the increase, driven by a demand for fuel from the towns and cities that could be reached by small ships sailing out of the South Wales ports.

Even so, such industries were a very minor feature of the Welsh economy in 1800. Fewer than 10 per cent of workers earned a living in industry. Agriculture, and especially cattle and sheep breeding, still dominated Wales — but not for long. King Coal was on his way.

Chapter Eight

King Coal

Industry in Wales

The Industrial Revolution came to Wales when businessmen from Lancashire were looking around for places to build new factories. Nearby areas of Wales seemed ideal. A pottery opened at Buckley in 1757, and within 20 years another 14 potteries opened near the town. A cotton mill opened at Holywell in 1777 and another at Mold in 1792. Thereafter cotton works sprang up across the area.

In 1761 John Wilkinson, who owned an ironworks at Bersham, began to sink coalmines near Chirk. Coal was essential to the iron-making process, so producing iron and coal together in one business was very efficient, and dozens of other firms in North Wales followed his example. Meanwhile, copper was being mined and smelted around Amlwch and Holywell, employing thousands of men. By 1820 Wales would produce 90% of all copper in Britain.

Slate

Slate quarrying began on a very small scale, with individual miners working by themselves. Then Richard Pennant decided to quarry slate on his huge estates around Caernarfon. By 1792 he was employing 500 men in the quarry and producing 15,000 tonnes of roofing slates a year. Other landowners followed his lead and by 1820 most of the slates used in Britain and America were coming from North Wales.

In 1798 Pennant, now Lord Penrhyn, invested in a horse-drawn railway to move slates to his specially built Port Penrhyn. Soon a network of narrow-gauge tracks wound through the hills from quarries to ports. In the 1860s many of these were converted into steam railways.

King Coal

The slate industry was founded and owned by Welsh landowners and worked by local Welshmen. As a result, it remained mainly Welsh-speaking. The industry kept the local North Wales population in work. The quarrying village of Blaenau Ffestiniog boomed from 732 people in 1801 to 11,274 in 1881. In the same year, the Welsh slate industry hit its peak with 355,000 tonnes of slates being exported. The huge boom in housebuilding across Europe fed the trade.

Underground art

During World War II, art treasures from the National Gallery, the Tate Gallery and the royal palaces were evacuated to North Wales so they would be safe from the bombing. They were stored in six air-conditioned chambers inside the Manod slate quarry at Blaenau Ffestiniog.

"Careful with that one, George. I'd say that was an early Rembrandt."

A very modern castle

Having made a fortune from his slate quarries, Richard Pennant got himself the title of Lord Penrhyn and began building Penrhyn Castle. Some helpful historians discovered that Prince Rhodri Molwynog ap Idwal of Gwynedd might have lived on this spot in about 720.

Despite appearing to be a medieval fortress from the outside, it was built with all the very latest modern conveniences. The castle is now open to the public.

The Ladies of Llangollen

In 1780 two unusual ladies came to live at Llangollen. Eleanor Butler and Sarah Ponsonby came from rich Irish families and shared a deep love of literature and the arts. Neither wanted to marry, so they scraped together enough money to rent an estate and came to the Welsh town to escape their disapproving relatives. They lived in Llangollen until their deaths in 1829 and 1832 respectively. Their learning and lifestyle attracted many visitors and they were given a pension by King George III. Their house, Plas Newydd, is now a museum.

By rail to Ffestiniog

In 1836 the Festiniog Railway opened to carry slate from the quarries near Blaenau Ffestiniog down to the harbour at Porthmadog. The line ceased working in 1939 as the demand for slate fell. But in 1955 it was reopened as a tourist attraction and it remains popular to this day.

The line is almost 22 kilometres long and runs on a narrow gauge of 59.7 centimetres. Steam locomotives, some of them dating from the 1860s, haul passenger carriages through some of the finest scenery in Wales.

Coal

But it was in the south-east that Welsh industrialisation really took hold, and that Welsh society, politics and economics moved into the modern age.

Underneath the ground of South Wales, covering a roughly oval area stretching from Llanelli in the west to Pontypool in the east and from Maesteg in the south to Brynmawr in the north, was a huge coalfield. In a few places the coal seam reached the surface, but in most places it was deep underground. Nobody doubted the high quality of this coal, nor the quantities in which it existed. It was the cost of getting it out of the ground that had put people off mining it. In the northern parts there was also iron ore to be found.

This underground treasure was overlain by limestone, which gave the area its characteristic hills covered in poor grazing land. It was later to be used to build the towns and cities that sprang up here.

Children in the mines

Until 1842, children as young as 5 years old went down the mines to work up to 12-hour shifts. The jobs the younger children were given included opening and closing trap doors to allow men and coal to pass through, then shutting them again for safety reasons or to control the airflow through the mine. Such children were called 'trappies'. After 1842, children under 10 were forbidden to go underground. Boys aged 10 and over continued to work underground for another 50 years.

Trappie works the doors

Bearer carries the coal

Putter loads the wagons

Drawer pulls them

The five worst mining disasters

1. **439 killed** at the Universal Colliery in Senghenydd on 14 October 1913 by an explosion of firedamp (flammable gas) and coal dust.

2. **290 killed** at the Albion Colliery in Cilfynydd on 23 June 1894 by an explosion of firedamp and coal dust.

3. **268 deaths** at the Prince of Wales Mine in Abercarn, 11 September 1878. A firedamp explosion was followed by fires that burned for two months.

4. **266 deaths** at the Gresford Colliery in Wrexham, 22 September 1934. A firedamp explosion was followed by asphyxiation after ventilation shafts collapsed.

5. **178 killed** at the Ferndale pit in the Rhondda, 8 November 1867, by a firedamp explosion.

The Song of Abercarn

In the village of Abercarn a colliery stands,
As safe 'twas supposed, as any in the land.
For several years, they had been free from harm,
No reason for trouble, no cause for alarm;
But death comes so silent down in the dark mine.
In the bowels of the earth, the sun cannot shine.
In the Abercarn Pit, men working for bread
In a moment were laid disfigured and dead.

Agricultural societies

During the 19th century, food imports to Britain from the Americas and Asia increased. As a result, prices for grain and meat fell. Many farmers in Wales went out of business, unprofitable land was abandoned and rural unemployment soared. In response, Welsh farmers formed a number of agricultural societies, which aimed to improve farming practices, put pressure on politicians and provide assistance to farming families. In 1904 the Royal Welsh Agricultural Society was founded; it has led Welsh farming ever since.

Country to town

In 1851, 35% of Welshmen worked on farms and 10% in coalmines. In 1911, 10% worked on farms and 35% in coalmines. In those 60 years Wales had changed from a rural nation to one dominated by towns. Most important were the towns of the South Wales coalfield, which, by 1914, housed 1.1 million people out of 2.5 million in the whole of Wales. The towns offered better wages and more reliable employment than the countryside, although living conditions were often appalling.

Coal and choirs

In the 1820s some Welshmen living in industrial areas began to form glee clubs – small groups of singers performing short songs. By the 1870s the glee clubs had mostly changed into male-voice choirs featuring men only, though some also had boys to sing the highest parts. Soon nearly every village or mine had its own choir, and Welsh regiments also boasted choirs. In 1902 the London Welsh Choir was formed, and in 1978 the Hong Kong Welsh Choir was created, while Toronto gained a choir in 1995. Today, Welsh male choirs have an international reputation.

Iolo Morganwg

Born Edward Williams (1747-1826), Iolo Morganwg adopted his bardic name when in his forties. He trained as a stonemason, but was always interested in Welsh poetry, history and antiquarian manuscripts. In 1792 he founded the *Gorsedd*, the association of Welsh bards, and organised a ceremony at Primrose Hill, London. Morganwg published his own poetry, which sold well, but he did better when editing ancient manuscripts. His ideas were taken up by modern druids and made a big impression on Welsh historians and language experts. He claimed that the ancient druids had survived as medieval bards, but after his death it was found that many of the 'ancient' manuscripts he used to prove this were forgeries.

Land of My Fathers

The song 'Hen Wlad fy Nhadau' ('Land of my Fathers') was adopted by so many eisteddfodau as an opening song that by 1870 it had become an unofficial national anthem.

Mae hen wlad fy nhadau yn annwyl i mi,
Gwlad beirdd a chantorion, enwogion o fri;
Ei gwrol ryfelwyr, gwladgarwyr tra mâd,
Dros ryddid gollasant eu gwaed.

(Cytgan:)

Gwlad, Gwlad, pleidiol wyf i'm gwlad.*
Tra môr yn fur i'r bur hoff bau,
O bydded i'r hen iaith barhau.

The old land of my fathers is dear to me,
Land of poets and singers, famous men of renown;
Her brave warriors, most splendid patriots,
For freedom shed their blood.

(Chorus:)

Nation, Nation, I pledge to my nation.
While the sea is a wall to the pure, most loved land,
O may the old language endure

---

* *The phrase 'Pleidiol wyf i'm gwlad' used to appear around the edge of some British £1 coins.*

The ten industrial valleys

1. **Ebbw Vale** boomed after an ironworks was opened there in 1778. It now has a population of 19,600, but the ironworks closed in 2003.

2. **Sirhowy Valley** was a major coalmining area. In 1978 it was the subject of a song by Welsh singer Max Boyce.

3. **Rhymney Valley** is now largely a commuter settlement for people working in Cardiff.

4. **The Taff Valley** runs from Merthyr Tydfil to Cardiff.

5. **The Cynon Valley** had the last deep coalmine operating in Wales: the Tower Colliery, which shut in 2008.

6. The twin **Rhondda Valleys** have the largest population, with about 70,000 residents.

7. **The Ely River** was the most polluted in Wales until it was cleaned up in 1980.

8. **The Tawe Valley** is dominated by Swansea (known in Welsh as Abertawe).

9. **The Ogmore** is now a leading fishing river for salmon and trout.

10. **Neath** is called the Waterfall Valley due to the large number of such falls.

Saving the language

In 1800 more than three-quarters of the population of Wales spoke Welsh and most of the rest knew something of the language. By 1900 only 43% spoke Welsh fluently, and around 25% knew no Welsh at all.

This was partly due to the spread of industry. Many of the terms used in mining and iron smelting were English, and many of the experts brought in to run the new businesses were English. Men found they needed to speak English at work, while teachers felt it essential to teach children in English if they were to succeed in a newly mobile world. Welsh fell into disuse in most industrial areas.

In 1865, 153 Welsh settlers arrived in Patagonia, Argentina, to found a new community where their language and way of life would be safe from English influence. The community, known as Y Wladfa ('the homeland'), is now 20,000 strong.

Sailing to Y Wladfa

Some mining words and phrases

bell Any smooth-sided, large stone which could fall from the roof without warning.

bumper A loud thud, which could cause equipment in a mine to shake. Bumpers are believed to be caused by the rock strata (layers) above the coal seam settling after the removal of the coal. For some reason bumpers were heard more often by the night shifts than the day shifts.

bunkin A soft layer of black shale often found underneath a coal seam in the South Wales coalfield. The word was sometimes used as a humorous name for cakes and puddings.

buttie Originally described a boy helping an older miner and learning the job; today it describes any workmate or friend.

button The man who operated the control button on the conveyor belt that carried coal away from the coalface. He was usually an older man, no longer fit enough for heavy manual work. The word later came to mean any man highly experienced at underground work.

clod A layer of soft rock found on the top of some coal seams.

haulier A man in charge of a pit pony.

hewer A man who worked at the coalface.

jump A place where the coal seam was displaced up or down by a fault in the rock strata.

muck Rock or waste mixed in with the coal seam.

podger A long steel bar pointed at one end and wedge-shaped at the other, generally used to prise out loose stones from walls or roofs.

pwkins A place where the floor of a passage has heaved up.
Red Indians Reddish-coloured cockroaches often found in mines.
squeeze A place where the roof of a passage deforms downwards, gradually breaking the pit props.
stent A section of coalface worked by a hewer in the days of hand hewing. It was usually about 8 to 10 yards (7-9 metres) in length.
Tommy box A tin box used for carrying sandwiches, rounded at one end for easier access into a pocket. The metal box was essential to stop the mice, rats or Red Indians from stealing the food.
toolbar A metal rod to which miners' tools were locked up at the end of each shift.

The phrase **The tools are on the bar** originally referred to the end of a shift, but was later used to refer to the end of any activity, and in particular the funeral of a miner.

A hewer at work

Wales A Very Peculiar History

Ironworking had been going on at Merthyr Tydfil on a small scale for generations, but it really took off after 1790. The canals built to carry iron also carried coal, and this made it worthwhile to export coal for the first time. From mines in the valleys the coal was taken to the ports, loaded onto ships and sent out across the world.

Railways replaced canals from 1840 onwards, giving the industries in the coalfields another huge boost. Even so, the iron industry was soon dwarfed by the coal business.

The railways incidentally created a new industry: the seaside resort. Vast numbers of families from industrial towns boarded trains to coastal resorts for their summer holidays. The world's first package deal of train ticket and hotel room was offered by Thomas Avin in Aberystwyth.

One reason the coal trade did so well, so quickly in South Wales is that landowners were paid a percentage of the value of any coal extracted from beneath their land. They were therefore more than happy to see railways, docks and workshops built on productive farmland in

King Coal

the valley bottoms. Since the landowners were the richest men in the region, it was often they who paid for these facilities and so reaped the profits. The Marquis of Bute, for instance, entirely rebuilt Cardiff Docks in 1839 at a cost of £350,000.

At first, most of the workers in the coalfield came from rural Wales. The towns and mines were generally Welsh-speaking, although most of the foremen and technical experts came from England. One result was that those in authority very often had no idea what the workers were talking about.

Taffy was a Welshman

The use of the name 'Taffy' as a slang term for a Welshman is first recorded in about 1720. It came either from the common Welsh name Dafydd (a Welsh form of 'David') or from the River Taff, on which Cardiff stands. Although many English people use it as a jocular term, it was used in a rude rhyme that begins 'Taffy was a Welshman, Taffy was a thief,' and is therefore viewed as an insulting term by some Welsh people.

Murmurs of dissent

In November of 1839, the authorities were caught by surprise by riots in Newport. These were linked to the Britain-wide Chartist movement — which called for reforms to Parliament and voting laws — but the exact aims of the hundreds of armed men who stormed into Newport are unclear. In the event they were poorly led and, after 20 had been killed by a squad of soldiers that happened to be present, the rioting subsided.

While the coalfields saw political unrest, the rural areas were the site of the Rebecca Riots. The men involved claimed to be the children of an imaginary 'Mother Rebecca' who wanted to go home but could not due to the tollgates erected across rural roads. The protests usually involved the destruction of tollgates, but attacks on other buildings that were thought to be unfair to farmers also took place. The farming industry was in a dire condition, with hundreds of Welsh farmers going bankrupt. The unemployed rural workers trudged to the growing industrial towns, swelling the workforce there.

King Coal

Bad as things were, the government could be relied upon to make them worse. Parliament ordered an inquiry into the state of education in Wales. The investigation was carried out by three men who spoke no Welsh, and their 1847 report caused outrage in Wales.

Known as the 'Blue Book', the report stated that the Welsh were poorly educated, mired in superstition and stuck in medieval lifestyles. The blame was put firmly on the Welsh language and Nonconformist religion. The outcry in Wales was immediate and angry. This anger soon found expression in the organising of eisteddfodau on a large scale for the first time in 300 years. In addition to many local events, a National Eisteddfod was held at Aberdare in 1861. The Welsh were determined to prove that they were as good as anyone else — especially the English fools who had written the Blue Book.

The feeling of separateness was also encouraged by religion. In Wales 66% of the population counted themselves as Nonconformists who attended a chapel on Sundays. The percentage of Nonconformists would rise over the next 40 years and may have reached 75%. Many

Nonconformists objected to paying taxes to support the Church of England.

Under British law at this time, the only people allowed to vote in elections were men who owned or rented property worth a certain amount. The booming prosperity of Wales had the unforeseen effect of greatly increasing the numbers of men who were eligible to vote. The political influence of landowners collapsed. In 1885 the constituency of the Rhondda elected a miner active in trades unionism named William 'Mabon' Abraham. At first he sat with the Liberals, but later he was to join the Labour Party. He is thus often said to have been the first Labour MP elected to the House of Commons.

The election of Mabon was a portent of things to come.

Chapter Nine

'Something Must Be Done'

For the first few years of the 20th century the booming prosperity of Welsh industry continued. Coal output increased by 58% between 1900 and 1914, and the iron industry also continued to expand.

But despite all this, problems were growing. The more easily worked seams of coal had been fully exploited and miners were having to move into the deeper, thinner seams that were more difficult and dangerous to extract. The mine owners did not invest in expensive machinery; it was cheaper just to send more men down the mines.

Wales A Very Peculiar History

In 1911, for the first time, Welsh speakers were in a minority in Wales. This was partly due to immigration from England, but there was also a feeling that the language was old-fashioned and outmoded. Those who spoke Welsh tended to feel that they were the only true Welsh people, though English-speakers with Welsh ancestors protested against this.

At the same time, attendance at Nonconformist chapels was on the decline, undermining a second traditional feature of Welshness. It appeared to many that Wales was becoming increasingly un-Welsh.

*David Lloyd George
1863-1945*

The 'Welsh Wizard' was the greatest orator of the early 20th century.

'Something Must Be Done'

Lloyd George

The greatest politician of the era was David Lloyd George, a fiery orator from Pembrokeshire (though born in Manchester) who entered Parliament in 1890 as Liberal MP for Caernarfon. Lloyd George entered the cabinet in 1906, leading a branch of the Liberal Party that favoured measures to help the poor. In 1911 he brought in a revolutionary budget that established a welfare state.

Then came the First World War, and everything changed.

Lloyd George became prime minister, leading a national coalition government, in 1916. When the war ended, he chose to stay on as prime minister, but relying on the support of the Conservative Party. At this time the trades unions in Welsh industrial areas were becoming more militant. Since many factory and mine owners were known Conservatives, many workers now abandoned the Liberals and supported the new Labour Party. In January 1919, representatives of the 271,000 miners in South Wales demanded more pay, shorter working hours and the nationalisation of coalmines, with miners making up 50% of the management team. They voted for a strike if they did not get what they wanted. This led to a Royal Commission on Coal which agreed with some of the miners' demands, but Lloyd George refused to act.

The fantasy village

In 1925 architect Sir Clough Williams-Ellis bought a disused boatyard and run-down cottages called Aber Iâ, renamed it Portmeirion and began building. He did not stop building until 1975, creating a bizarre fantasy village of Italianate design. Portmeirion is a grand hotel with with all the various buildings being bedrooms, restaurants or shops.

The village has been used as a setting for film and TV shows, often serving as a cheap alternative to filming in Italy. It was famously the backdrop for the surreal spy drama *The Prisoner*, made in 1967.

'Something Must Be Done'

Wales in decline

In 1921 the demand for coal slumped, mine owners cut wages and a strike began. It proved to be only the first in a series of bitter disputes that accompanied the decline of the coal industry. By 1941 the number of miners would be half what it had been in 1921, and by 1971 the numbers were barely 20% of the 1921 total.

As the coal industry declined, so did the iron business. The first plant to close was Cyfarthfa in 1921, but during the next fifteen years many other iron mills shut down. In the former coal and iron town of Brynmawr, unemployment peaked at 90%. As coal and iron declined, there was less for the railways and ports to do, so they shed workers and saw profits fall. Seaside resorts had fewer holidaymakers to cater for, so they lost prosperity too. It was a vicious circle.

In 1936 the new king, Edward VIII, made a visit to South Wales. He visited a number of families, social clubs and factories to see for himself the poverty and unemployment in the area. At Blaenafon he said, 'Something must be done.' The remark was overheard and reported by a newspaperman. The entire country agreed — but not on what it was that needed to be done.

In 1937 the government began paying subsidies to companies that were willing to set up factories in areas of high unemployment. At least 5,000 new jobs appeared in the coalfields.

While the 19th century had seen immigration to Wales, the twenty years after the First World War saw emigration. In all, 390,000 people left Wales, mostly for England, Australia or the USA. The trend would continue for most of the 20th century.

Welsh speaking was continuing to decline. In 1921 there were 156,000 people who spoke only Welsh but not English; ten years later there were 98,000 — though the number of people who spoke some Welsh had not fallen much at all. Many local authorities were reluctant to allow schools to teach in Welsh, in case the children's employment prospects were damaged by a lack of ability to speak English. Meanwhile, however, a small group of determined scholars and wealthy men led by W. J. Gruffydd encouraged a new age of Welsh literature.

'Something Must Be Done'

The Second World War struck Wales less severely than the First. Less than half as many Welshmen were killed in battle: 15,000 compared to 40,000. German bombing of industrial areas did inflict some civilian casualties. Swansea lost 230 in a single raid in February 1941, and the city centre was flattened. Many children were evacuated from the industrial towns to rural areas.

There was a positive side for Wales. The demand for armaments boosted the traditional industries of iron and coal, so that unemployment fell from 146,000 in 1939 to just 7,000 by 1944. At the same time, many factories in Wales were converted to new industries, which taught the workers new skills. These skills would come in useful after the war, when demand for coal and iron began to fall off.

An invented investiture

For centuries, kings of England had invested their eldest son as Prince of Wales by signing a legal document and giving them a coronet to wear. But in 1911 King George V wanted to show the importance that he attached to Wales, and insisted that a formal ceremony was needed when his son Edward became Prince of Wales. Caernarfon Castle was chosen as the venue and an entirely new ceremony was drawn up that was based on medieval precedents. In addition to the old coronet, a new ring, rod, sword, girdle and cloak were made. It all looked suitably medieval, but this was an entirely invented investiture. The 1969 investiture of Prince Charles (right) followed a similar pattern.

The missing coronet

When officials were planning the investiture of Prince Charles as Prince of Wales in 1969, they soon hit a snag. The Coronet of Wales, the formal headgear of the Prince of Wales, was missing! After he abdicated in 1936, Edward VIII had gone off with a number of royal jewels, including the coronet, and it was feared it had been melted down and the jewels sold. A new coronet was therefore made that was of starkly modern design. In 1972 the former king died and the coronet was found intact among his possessions. It was returned to the royal family, so Prince Charles now has a choice of two coronets. (He actually wears neither.)

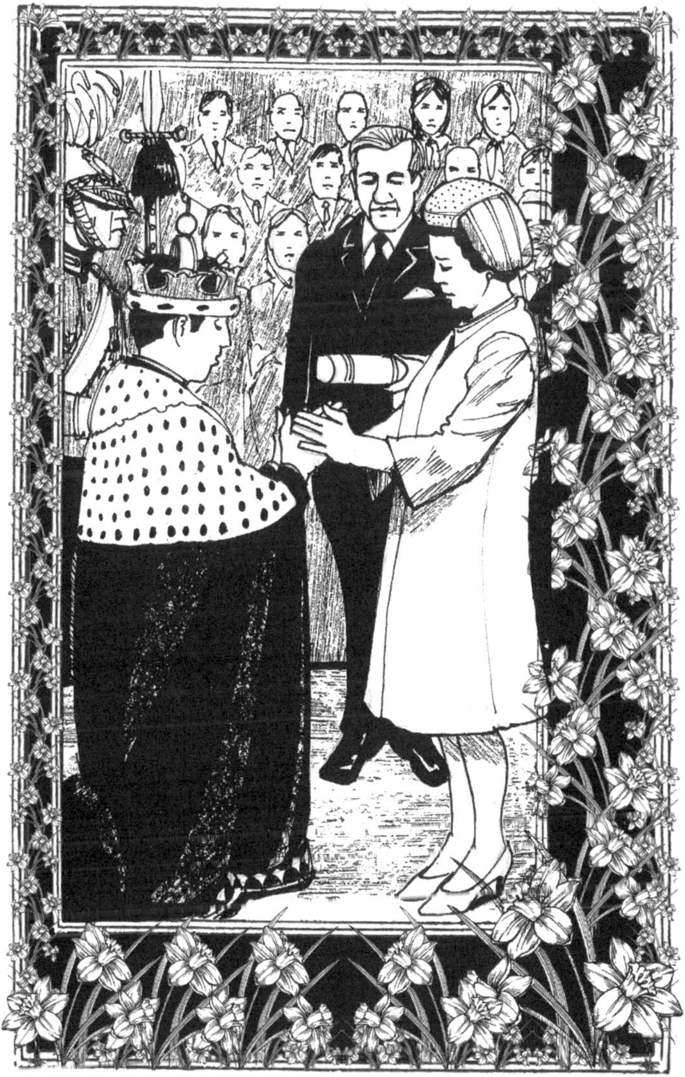

Hope at last?

At the postwar election of 1945, the industrial areas of Wales voted solidly Labour. Rural districts were divided between the Liberals and the Conservatives. The Labour government soon gave economic help to factories in Wales, and nationalisation of the coalmines and the iron and steel industries all served to help the prosperity of South Wales. It was a time of great hope in the coalfields. Miners had long blamed private owners and the capitalist system for the problems of the industry, and hoped that nationalisation would end them.

It proved to be a false hope. The underlying problems of the coalfields could not be solved by a change of management. Within three years of nationalisation, 34 pits were closed, and although new ones were opened they employed fewer men.

The iron industry seemed to offer more hope with the opening of huge new works at Margam, Trostre and Felindre. But unfortunately there was not much of a market for their products.

'Something Must Be Done'

By the 1960s the industrial workers of Wales were being kept in employment largely by government money. The boom days had gone.

There was also a growing feeling that Wales was not getting a fair deal from the British government. Some people, especially the members of Plaid Cymru (see page 158), objected to the building of military bases in the Principality. However, worse was to come with the flooding of the Tryweryn Valley.

In 1957 the British parliament voted to build a dam that would flood the Tryweryn Valley to create a reservoir for the English city of Liverpool – although nearly every Welsh MP voted against it. There followed protests and violent attacks on the dam works, but the work went ahead. It was partly because of this that Plaid Cymru managed to get its first member into parliament.

Nevertheless, the 1960s drew to a close with a growing feeling in Wales that Welshness was under threat and that the country got a raw deal from the UK.

Plaid Cymru

On 5 August of 1925, a new political party was formed with the twin aims of making Welsh the only official language in Wales and promoting Welsh home rule under a Welsh government.

Plaid Cymru (the Party of Wales) got its first MP at the 1966 by-election in Carmarthen. In the 1974 election the party won three seats. After devolution in 1998, Plaid Cymru has done better at elections to the Welsh Assembly than to Westminster.

Cymdeithas yr Iaith Gymraeg

Founded in 1962, Cymdeithas yr Iaith Gymraeg (the Welsh Language Society) aims to use non-violent means to further the use and status of the Welsh language.

Several early demands – such as making Welsh an official language and starting a Welsh- language TV station – have been met. The Society now wants to make private companies use Welsh and English equally, as the government now does in Wales.

Over the years more than a thousand members and supporters have appeared in court for minor offences such as daubing graffiti on walls, obstructing roads, invading TV studios and damaging property.

Mudiad Amddiffyn Cymru

Also known as MAC or Movement for the Defence of Wales, this organisation was set up in 1963 and was modelled on the IRA (Irish Republican Army).

Its first act was to plant a bomb at an electricity transformer. This was followed by a bombing campaign against English-owned businesses. In 1969 the group set off bombs to coincide with the investiture of Prince Charles as Prince of Wales. Two MAC members were killed. In 1970 the group's leader was convicted of the bombings, and the organisation fell apart while he was in prison.

The tragedy of Aberfan

At 9.15 a.m. on 21 October, 1966, a huge tip of mining waste collapsed down the side of Merthyr Mountain. Travelling at high speed in a wall over 15 metres high, hundreds of thousands of tonnes of mud and rock smashed into the village of Aberfan, demolishing 22 houses and the Pantglas Junior School. Villagers raced to the site, soon joined by police and thousands more volunteers from nearby villages who dug desperately to rescue those trapped. A few were saved, but 144 people died – 116 of them schoolchildren. New laws about waste tips were introduced as a result. A memorial now stands on the site of the school.

King of Hay-on-Wye

Hay-on-Wye was just a small market town until 1961, when Richard Booth opened a second-hand bookshop in the old fire station. The shop was so successful that other bookshops opened in the town and it became a major destination for collectors of rare books.

On 1 April, 1977, Booth declared the town to be an independent kingdom with himself as king, and organised a series of publicity stunts that boosted even further the number of visitors. Since 1988 an annual literary festival has been held in Hay for ten days in May, attracting up to 80,000 visitors to events that include musical and theatrical performances.

"Is it a first edition? I'm slightly foxed."

Chapter Ten

Into the Future

Since 1970 Wales has been reborn in an economic and cultural explosion unlike any other. Some date the new Wales to 1955, when the government agreed to stop saying 'England' when it meant 'England and Wales', and when Cardiff became the capital of Wales.

There was a strong new feeling that Wales and the Welsh were special. This nationalism boosted the success of Plaid Cymru, which consistently won three or four MPs at general elections from 1974 onwards. There was also growing support for some form of home rule.

Wales A Very Peculiar History

In 1972 the Conservative government swept away the English-style counties in Wales. In their place were eight large counties, some of them reviving the names of ancient Welsh principalities. The next Labour government put forward a plan for a Welsh Assembly which would have limited powers. The plan was rejected by Welsh voters.

In 1984 the National Coal Board announced that a number of unprofitable pits were to be closed. Many people in South Wales feared that the poverty of the 1930s would return. The head of the National Union of Miners, Arthur Scargill, called for a strike. The strike dragged on for almost a year before the miners realised that the government was not going to change its plans.

The results of the strike were widespread. The powers of trades unions were abolished, nationalised industries were privatised and government subsidies were cut dramatically. In industrial areas of Wales, many felt that the government in London did not care for Welsh interests. This fuelled support for devolution both in Wales and in the Labour Party.

Into the Future

What'll we do now? It's the pits!

The seven-foot leek

In 1970 former miner Max Boyce took to writing comic songs and performing them in the social clubs of South Wales. In 1973 a performance at Treorchy Rugby Club was recorded and the recording went gold. His next album became the only comedy record to hit No. 1 in the charts. His blend of comedy, sentiment, devotion to rugby and outrageous Welshness – he appeared on stage with a giant leek – proved to be a national hit. He made Welshness fashionable across the UK.

A new start

When a new Labour government was elected in 1997, one of its first acts was to introduce new plans for a Welsh Assembly. These were approved by a tiny majority (support was greatest in Welsh-speaking areas), and the Assembly met for the first time in 1998. Its powers were fairly limited, but were widened in 2006.

An unforeseen effect of devolution was to break the grip of the Labour Party on Welsh politics. An increasing number of representatives from other parties found themselves in the Assembly. At the same time, there was a dramatic fall in the number of Labour MPs who had worked in manual industries.

At this time, many powers were being taken from the UK by the European Union (EU). Plaid Cymru now abandoned its policy of wanting Wales to be an independent nation state, and instead began to call for Wales to be a member state of the EU on a par with the UK.

Where's the dragon?

The flag of the United Kingdom, the Union Flag or Union Jack, is a combination of the red cross of St George for England, the white saltire (diagonal cross) of St Andrew for Scotland and the red saltire of St Patrick for Ireland – but there is no Welsh dragon.

This is because when the flag was designed in 1801, Wales was legally part of England and so was represented by the English flag. The Welsh dragon flag (see page 15), which was adopted in 1959, could not easily be fitted into the Union Jack. In recent years, however, there has been a move to make the Cross of St David the flag of Wales. This is a gold cross on a black field, and could more easily be included in a revised Union Jack.

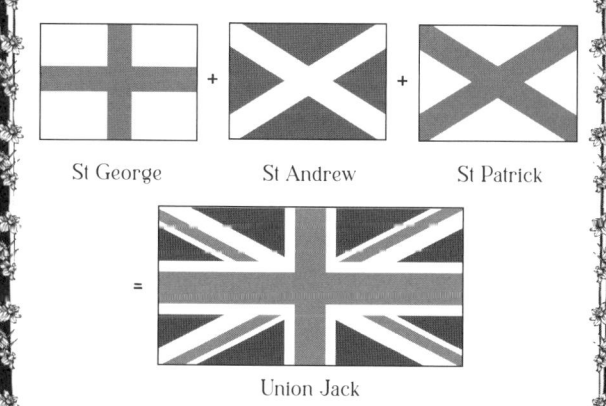

St George + St Andrew + St Patrick

= Union Jack

Scene of national pride

In 1970 Cardiff Arms Park was designated as the national sports stadium for Wales. Almost at once it came to be dominated by rugby, though other sports and musicians also used the venue. Players such as Barry John, Gareth Edwards and Phil Bennett dominated the ground as Wales won the Triple Crown seven times in 15 years and England failed to win – even once – at the ground. The passionate crowd, the massed singing and the seemingly endless run of success made the image of a jovial Welsh rugby fan a popular one across the world.

In 1997 the stadium was replaced by the much larger Millennium Stadium. The first event there was a rugby match that saw Wales beat South Africa with 29-19.

Hitting the high notes

In recent years two soprano singers have become major media celebrities. Charlotte Church reached No. 1 in the record charts aged just 12. Her early work was classical, but she later turned to pop and TV chat shows.

Katherine Jenkins released her first classical album in 2004 at the age of 24. She is now one of the world's most successful classical singers and a ambassador for many charities. With numerous number-one albums behind her, she has also starred in West End, film and TV roles, and taken part in many events hosted by the British Royal Family.

Ten Welsh people in the public eye

1. **Timothy Dalton**, film actor. Best known for his role as James Bond.

2. **Dawn French**, actress and comedienne. Star of the TV series *The Vicar of Dibley*.

3. **Jonathan Pryce CBE**, actor. Famous for playing sinister villains in Hollywood movies.

4. **Catherine Zeta Jones**, actress. She won an Oscar for her role as Velma Kelly in the 2002 film musical *Chicago*.

5. **Sir Anthony Hopkins CBE**, actor. Famous for his Oscar-winning role as Hannibal Lecter. Hopkins received a star on the Hollywood Walk of Fame in 2003.

6. **Michael Sheen**, actor recognized for his roles in *Frost/Nixon*, *The Queen*, and *Masters of Sex*.

7. **John Humphrys**, journalist. Well known for grilling politicians in TV interviews.

8. **Simon Weston CBE**, soldier, broadcaster and a veteran of the Falklands War of 1982.

9. **Dame Shirley Bassey CH DBE**, singer. She has sold 140 million records and is noted for her renditions of James Bond theme tunes.

10. **Sir Tom Jones OBE**, singer. His real name is Thomas Woodward. The legendary heart-throb has sold 400 million records worldwide.

The revival of Welsh

The Welsh language was also undergoing change. In previous generations immigrants, mostly English, had moved to industrialised areas of Wales, causing the language to decline there. From 1950 onwards the majority of immigrants from England moved to rural areas where they sought improved quality of life. The few remaining areas where Welsh was the everyday language now began to show a marked decline in the percentage of residents who still had Welsh as their first language.

The new influx of English families to Welsh-speaking areas sparked a rash of protests and violent incidents. The most notorious of these were the cottage burnings. In December of 1979 a cottage owned by an English family went up in flames as a result of arson. Some 220 others were to follow, most of them empty holiday homes. A group calling itself Meibion Glyndŵr, or Sons of Glyndŵr, said they were responsible. Nobody was ever convicted of the attacks, which ceased in the early 1990s.

Into the Future

More peaceful clashes came over education. English-speaking pupils at Welsh-speaking schools were at a disadvantage, and vice-versa. The answer at first seemed to be to have separate lessons, but later separate schools were opened. Eventually Welsh became a compulsory subject at English-speaking schools. This ensured that all children in Wales had some knowledge of Welsh, even if they were far from fluent.

For once, the percentage of Welsh-speakers began to rise. From 18.9% in 1981 it grew to 21% by 2001. In addition to those fluent in the language, another 34% had some knowledge of Welsh.

As the study of Welsh intensified, the fact that there are two main dialects of the language became obvious. The North Wales dialect, in particular that of the north-west, was highly valued as being less contaminated by English. Literature came increasingly to be written in a formal version of North Welsh. The dialect of South Wales is, however, equally valid as a spoken language and continues to develop, as any living language must.

Wales A Very Peculiar History

As Welsh became more popular, the government began giving grants to Welsh publishers. The number of books published in Welsh annually doubled between 1973 and 1990. In these same years a number of colleges set up theatres to keep alive the tradition of performing Welsh plays. New works were penned by Gwynn ap Gwilym, Gereint Bowen, Marged Dafydd and Bobi Jones.

Welsh place names

Welsh place names often reveal something of the history or geography of the location. *Aber*, for instance, is one of the most common beginnings for a coastal Welsh place name. It means 'mouth of a river'. *Afon*, on the other hand, refers to a river itself. *Caer* indicates a fortified building of stone and *Dinas* a fortified place of any kind. *Porth* means a harbour. *Llan* is the word for a church, and in place names is usually followed by the name of the saint to whom the local church is dedicated; the very common name *Llanfair* means 'St Mary's'.

Some handy Welsh phrases

Bore da (**BOH**-reh **DAH**) Good morning.

Croeso i Gymru (**CROY**-so ee **GUM**-ree) Welcome to Wales.

Da iawn (**DAH** ee-**YOWN**) Very good.

Diolch (**DEE**-olch*) Thanks.

Dw i ddim eisiau cinio (doo ee thim EH-shy **KIN**-your) I don't want any lunch.

Esgusodwch fi (esk-ee-**SO**-dooch* **VEE**) Excuse me.

Ga i un? (**GUY** een) Can I have one?

Iechyd da! (**YEH**-chi*-**DAH**) Cheers!

Mae hi'n oer (my **HIN** oir) It's cold.

Nos da (**NOS** dah) Goodnight.

Noswaith da (**NOS**-wythe **DAH**) Good evening.

Parti gwisg ffansi (party **GWEE**-sig fancy) Fancy-dress party.

Prynhawn da (Prin-**HOWN DAH**) Good afternoon.

Rwyt ti eisiau bag coch gydar ffrog (roo-**EE**- tee EH-shy bag koch* **GUH** dar frog) You want a red bag with the dress.

Tafarn (**TAV**-arn) Pub.

* see page 180 for pronounciation

The rise of Wenglish

Since the 1950s the form of English spoken in Wales has come to be recognised as a distinct dialect of the language. In addition to the Welsh accent, 'Wenglish' has the following features:

- Intonation goes up at the ends of sentences.

- A word is emphasised by putting it at the start of a sentence: 'Big it is,' for example.

- Repetition of a word is used to give emphasis. For example, in Welsh, you might say "Mae'r paent yn goch goch" to emphasize that the paint is very red, which directly translates to 'The paint is red red' in English.

- Some vowels and syllables may be pronounced longer than in England.

- 'Isn't it?' is used where English people would say 'didn't I?', 'haven't they?', etc.

- 'Is it?' is used to make a question: 'Going shopping, is it?'

The speaking of Wenglish goes back a long way. Shakespeare has some of his characters use the dialect. Fluellen in *Henry V*, for instance, says 'looke you' several times, and he puts a word at the start of a sentence for emphasis. 'Fluellen', of course, is an English person's attempt to say 'Llywelyn'.

Into the Future

Time and space and Cardiff

Perhaps the most popular performing art based in Wales is the series of *Doctor Who* shows made in Cardiff by BBC Wales.

After running continuously since 1963, the first *Doctor Who* series was cancelled amid much controversy in 1990. In September 2003 it was announced that a new series was to be made, and filming began in Cardiff in July the following year. It made it to TV screens in March 2005. It was an immediate hit and the show continues to be made.

Although made in Wales, the programme is rarely set there. Very different was the spin-off show *Torchwood*, which centres on a top-secret scientific establishment located beneath Cardiff. The show deliberately shows Wales as a dynamic, modern country, without any of the old stock characters in sight — apart from a single ex-miner.

The CAT of Machynlleth

The Centre for Alternative Technology (CAT) was opened in the disused Llwyngwern slate quarry at Machynlleth in 1974, long before environmentalism was fashionable. It was the brainchild of Gerard Morgan-Grenville, a wealthy businessman with an interest in nature and environmental issues. It was once a tourist attraction and is now a centre for group and educational visits.

All the water at CAT comes from the surrounding hills. It is used for generating energy, running the cliff railway, watering plants, providing habitats for wildlife, drinking (after going through a chemical-free purification process), cooking and washing. Water conservation measures include compost toilets, water-saving nozzles on the taps, and displays to demonstrate how you can reduce water usage in your home and garden.

The cliff railway is one of the steepest in the world, with a gradient of 35 degrees. There are two carriages linked together with a steel cable, so that when one carriage goes down the other is pulled up. It is operated by means of water tanks located under each carriage. When the tank on one carriage is filled, the weight of the water pulls that carriage gently down, raising the other. The water is then emptied out of the tank, and the tank on the other carriage is filled to repeat the process.

Unusual construction methods are used to minimise the impact buildings have on the environment. The old quarry buildings were renovated with local stone. Buildings put up since have used timber frames and local materials such as straw and rammed earth. Turf roofs have been used to provide a home for insects and birds. Solar power and water power are used to provide energy for heating and other uses.

The WISE building holds the Wales Institute for Sustainable Development. It is constructed to the highest standard of 'green' building and incorporates a range of traditional and innovative construction techniques. It contains teaching rooms, laboratories and a lecture theatre.

For the less ambitious, the Eco-House includes tips and demonstrations on how to be kind to the environment in your own home on a daily basis. Eco-friendly domestic appliances and household products are included, along with ways to reduce power consumption. There is also a garden designed to provide natural habitats for birds and animals, composting and rainwater harvesting facilities and space for growing food.

In addition to the displays open to the public, the CAT is home to the Graduate School of the Environment and hosts a variety of courses lasting from a few hours to several days.

Getting to the top

The highest point in Wales is the summit of Yr Wyddfa (Mount Snowdon) at 1,085 metres. The first known climber was the naturalist Thomas Johnson, who scrambled up in 1639. There are now several recognised routes to the summit. The Crib Goch is probably the most difficult and should not be attempted in winter or by inexperienced climbers. The Llanberis Path is longer, but involves nothing more arduous than some uphill walking. Easiest of all is the Snowdon Mountain Railway that runs from Llanberis to the summit, where there is a restaurant and a shop.

The four most visited castles in Wales

1. **Caernarfon.** Begun on the orders of Edward I in 1285, but not completed until 1327. The unusual polygonal towers and banded stonework were copied from the walls of Constantinople (Istanbul). It last saw action in 1646, and restoration was begun in 1908. It now houses the museum of the Royal Welch Fusiliers.

2. **Conwy.** This was the most expensive of the castles built by Edward I, having a price tag of £22,000. The castle survived intact until 1660 when the Earl of Conway* stripped it of anything valuable – including the roofs.

3. **Harlech.** This mighty fortress survived only because the heavy rains of 1647 made it impossible for Parliament's General Mytton to bring his heavy artillery along the winding mountain roads to smash the walls to pieces. The Royalist Garrison surrendered when hunger forced them.

4. **Beaumaris.** The most perfect concentric castle in Britain, Beaumaris was so strong that it was never attacked.

* the English name for Conwy

Gold from the hills

Welsh gold is traditionally used to make wedding rings for royal brides. There are three main gold mines in Wales:

1. **Dolaucothi**, near Pumpsaint, Dyfed, was run by the Romans, then reopened in the Victorian era, but it closed in 1938. It is now open again as a museum.

2. **Gwynfynydd** in Dolgellau opened in the 1860s and produced at least 45,000 ounces (1.3 million grams) in its heyday from the late 1800s to early 1900s.

3. **Clogau** at Bontddu near Barmouth opened in 1862 and was the largest gold mine in Wales and the UK's biggest gold producer, yielding over 80,000 ounces of gold before closing in 1998. The ore is not very rich and the mine is closed until it can be extracted profitably again.

Cardiff Bay development

The redevelopment of 1,100 hectares of derelict industrial land around Cardiff Bay has proved to be one of the most outstanding regeneration projects in Britain. Work began in 1987 and continues today. Among the best-known buildings on the site are the Millennium Centre opera house, the *Senedd* or debating chamber for the Welsh Assembly, the Roald Dahl Plass open amphitheatre and the Techniquest educational science centre. The development has featured in *Doctor Who* and other TV shows, drawing attention to the dynamic and modern face of Wales in the 21st century.

Wales looks to the future

As the 21st century continues, Wales is an optimistic country. It has its own Assembly and government, its language is secure and the economy is recovering from its troubles better than many other areas.

Wales may have had a very peculiar history, but it looks set for a great future.

Pronouncing Welsh

Here is a rough guide to Welsh pronunciation for English speakers. It won't make you sound like a native, but should help you to make yourself understood if you need to ask directions.

There are 28 letters in the Welsh alphabet:

a b c ch d dd e f ff g ng h i l ll m n o p ph r rh s t th u w y

The letters j, k, q, v, x, z are used only in foreign words. Some people may tell you that many Welsh words have no vowels; this is not true, because both **w** and **y** are vowels in Welsh. Many letters are pronounced much the same as in English, but some are very different:

a is an 'ah' sound, never like 'a' in 'make'.
c is always a 'k' sound, never an 's' sound.
ch is pronounced as in 'loch'.
dd is like 'th' in 'this' (**not** like 'th' in 'thin').
e is like the first part of 'a' in 'make', never 'ee'.
f is like English 'v'. At the end of a word it is often silent.
ff is like English 'f'.
i is like a short 'ee', never like 'eye'; when followed by another vowel, it becomes a consonant like English 'y'.
ll is a sound that doesn't exist in English, rather like an 'h' and an 'l' pronounced at the same time. If you say 'hl' you won't sound very Welsh, but you'll be understood.

Pronouncing Welsh

r is like the first part of a trilled or rolled 'r'.

rh is similar, but accompanied with an 'h' sound.

s is always an 's' sound, never a 'z' sound; but **si** before a vowel is like English 'sh': Welsh **siop** = English 'shop'.

th is like 'th' in 'thin' (**not** like 'th' in 'this').

u is 'ee' — a confusing one for English speakers.

w is sometimes a vowel, 'oo', and sometimes a consonant like English 'w'. In the word **gwlad** (see page 137) it's a consonant, so this word has only one syllable.

y is sometimes pronounced 'ee', especially when it's in the last syllable of a word. A other times it's an 'uh' sound, somewhere between 'u' in 'but' and 'e' in 'father'.

ae, ai, au, ei, eu, ey all sound very similar, rather like English 'eye'.

oe is like English 'oi' or 'oy'.

wy is like 'oo-ee', but pronounced as one syllable.

yw is like 'ee-oo', but pronounced as one syllable.

A circumflex accent, as in **tân** ('fire'), indicates a long vowel sound.

Words of more than one syllable are usually stressed on the last syllable but one.

It's unusual for outsiders to become proficient in Welsh, but Welsh speakers will appreciate it if you make some effort.

Wales A Very Peculiar History

Glossary

abdicate To give up being king or queen.

arson The crime of setting fire to buildings.

auxiliaries Soldiers in the Roman army who were not Roman citizens.

bard A traditional Celtic poet.

bilingual Able to speak two languages equally well.

Brythonic The language spoken by the Celtic peoples of southern Britain before c. AD 450.

by-election A local election, as opposed to a national one.

chronicle A history of past events year by year.

civitas An area of local government in Roman times.

coalition A government with members from more than one party working together.

Cymru The Welsh name for Wales.

Cymry The Welsh name for themselves.

devolution A kind of partial independence, in which part of a state (such as Wales) has powers over itself, but not over the rest of the state (such as the other countries of the UK).

druid A priest and wise man in pagan Celtic society.

eisteddfod (plural **eisteddfodau**) A Welsh festival of song, poetry and other arts.

gorsedd A group of bards, especially one that meets to organise an eisteddfod or other event.

gwely An extended family group in medieval Wales.

gwelyau The land owned by a gwely.

home rule A system in which a country (such as Wales) rules itself, rather than being ruled by a more powerful country (such as the UK).

Glossary

legion A unit in the Roman army composed of around 6,000 professional Roman soldiers.

manuscript A book or document written by hand.

marcher lords English lords who tried to rule the Welsh Marches in medieval times.

Marches, the The borderland between Wales and England.

Nonconformist A person who does not agree with the majority view, especially a Christian who does not belong to the official Church of a country.

overlord A medieval lord who had limited powers over lesser lords.

pagan Following a religion other than Christianity, Judaism or Islam.

prince An independent ruler in Wales in medieval times, equivalent to an English king.

principality The land ruled by a prince.

Principality, the Another name for Wales.

repeal To cancel (a law).

seam A layer of coal under the ground.

smelting Heating a mineral (such as iron ore) to extract a more useful mineral (such as iron).

subsidy Money given by the government to help out an industry or other organisation.

usurper A person who takes over a position or title that rightfully belongs to another.

Valleys, the An industrialised area of South Wales.

villa A large farming estate attached to a country house in Roman times.

welfare state A system in which public money is used to provide services (such as education or health care) for those who cannot afford to pay for them.

Timeline of Welsh history

c.250,000 BC Pontnewydd Man: oldest known human remains in Wales.
c.5500 BC Forests spread across Wales.
c.4000 BC First evidence of farming in Wales.
c.2200 BC Beaker culture appears.
c.2000 BC Copper is smelted in Wales for the first time, and used to make tools.
c.1400 BC Climate becomes cooler and wetter. Villages begin to be fortified.
c.1000 BC Construction of hillforts begins.
c.500 BC Celtic culture spreads across Wales.
AD 43 Roman invasion of Britain begins.
49 Roman XX Legion is based at Gloucester to watch tribes in Wales.
51 Ordovices defeated by Romans.
52 Silures defeat a Roman invasion.
57 Roman invasion of Wales called off due to the rebellion of Boudicca (Boadicea) in eastern Britain.
75 Silures defeated by Romans.
c.75 Gold mining begins at Dolaucothi.
82 Ordovices defeated by Romans; Roman conquest of Wales completed.
c.260 Towns begin to erect defensive walls.
c.320 A major naval base is built at Cardiff.
367 The 'Barbarian Conspiracy': raiders overrun much of Britain, but are driven off.
c.390 Niall of the Nine Hostages raids Britain from his base in Ireland.
c.390 Cunedda is appointed to defend northern Wales. His descendants become rulers in the area.

Timeline of Welsh history

410 Roman Emperor Honorius tells Britain to look after its own defence.

c.420 British *civitates* elect Vortigern as ruler of post-Roman Britain

c.440 Germanic mercenaries led by brothers Hengist and Horsa rebel against Vortigern and grab Kent as the first English kingdom.

c.470 Ambrosius Aurelianus takes over from Vortigern.

c.490–530 Arthur is the leading figure in post-Roman Britain.

c.520 Birth of St David who reformed Christian monasticism in Wales.

c.550 Post-Roman government collapses. Power in Wales is seized by a number of rulers, who come to be called 'princes'.

616 Battle of Chester: an English victory that secures most of Britain for the invaders.

c.770 The area ruled by Welsh princes is reduced to about that of modern Wales.

c.780 Offa's Dyke built to divide England from Wales.

844 Rhodri Mawr becomes Prince of Gwynedd.

904 Hywel Dda becomes Prince of Deheubarth.

c.930 Hywel Dda formulates his law code.

986 Maredudd ap Owain unites most of Wales under his rule.

1055 Prince Gruffydd ap Llywelyn burns Hereford and captures border areas from England.

1057 Gruffydd ap Llywelyn becomes the first and last prince to unite all of Wales under his rule.

1093 The Welsh principality of Brycheiniog becomes the English lordship of Brecon, marking the start of the Norman takeover of southern Wales.

1094 Morgannwg, Brycheiniog and Buellt are captured by the Normans.

c.1100 The Mabinogion is compiled.

Wales A Very Peculiar History

1136 The Battle of Crug Mawr (or Cardigan) sees the Normans defeated.

1194 Llywelyn the Great becomes Prince of Gwynedd.

1267 The Treaty of Montgomery recognises Llywelyn the Last as Prince of Wales.

1282 Death of Llywelyn the Last.

1284 King Edward I begins the construction of the great castles of North Wales.

1294 Rebellion of Madog ap Llywelyn.

1315 Rebellion led by Llywelyn Bren.

1349 The Black Death devastates Wales.

1400–1412 Rebellion of Owain Glyndŵr.

1404 Glyndŵr calls a Parliament of Wales.

1485 Welsh nobleman Henry Tudor becomes King of England.

1535–1542 Laws in Wales Acts make Wales effectively part of the kingdom of England.

1588 The Morgan Bible is the first complete Bible to be published in Welsh.

1647 Harlech Castle surrenders to the Parliamentary forces in the Civil War and is partly demolished.

1761 John Wilkinson of Bersham is the first man to own both coalmines and ironworks.

1778 First steelworks opens in Ebbw Vale.

1792 Iolo Morganwg founds the Gorsedd of Bards.

1839 The Marquis of Bute rebuilds Cardiff Docks to cope with coal and iron exports.

1839 Chartist riots in Newport leave 20 dead.

1839–1842 Rebecca Riots rock rural areas.

1847 'Treason of the Blue Books': unrest over a report into education in Wales.

1861 The first National Eisteddfod is held at Aberdare.

Timeline of Welsh history

1870 'Hen Wlad fy Nhadau' (Land of my Fathers) becomes the unofficial Welsh national anthem.
1890 David Lloyd George becomes MP for Caernarfon.
1908 Penygraig miners' strike sparks national action.
1910 Tonypandy Riots leave one man dead and nearly 600 in hospital.
1911 Welsh-speakers are in a minority in Wales for the first time ever.
1913 Senghenydd mine disaster kills 439 miners, Britain's worst mine accident.
1914 Outbreak of World War I.
1916 Lloyd George becomes Prime Minister of Great Britain.
1919 Lloyd George sets up Royal Commission on Coal.
1920 Employment in the South Wales coalmines peaks at 271,000 miners.
1921 First major ironworks closure takes place at Cyfarthfa.
1922 Liberal Party reduced to two MPs in Wales.
1925 Plaid Cymru founded.
1936 King Edward VIII visits South Wales to view economic deprivation.
1937 The BBC sets up its Welsh Region.
1939 Outbreak of World War II leads to renewed demand for coal and iron.
1947 Coal industry nationalised.
1955 Wales is officially separated from England. Cardiff becomes the new national capital.
1958 Flooding of the Tryweryn Valley to create a reservoir for Liverpool sparks protests.
1959 The Welsh dragon flag is officially adopted.
1961 Richard Booth opens his first bookshop in Hay-on-Wye.
1962 Cymdeithas yr Iaith Gymraeg (Welsh Language Society) founded.

Wales A Very Peculiar History

1963 Mudiad Amddiffyn Cymru (Movement for the Defence of Wales) set up.

1966 Aberfan Disaster.

1970 Cardiff Arms Park is designated the national stadium for Welsh sport.

1972 English-style counties are replaced by regions with Welsh names.

1973 Max Boyce records his LP 'Live at Treorchy'.

1974 Plaid Cymru wins 3 MPs at the General Election.

1979 Campaign of arson against English-owned cottages in Wales.

1979 Wales votes against a Welsh Assembly.

1984–1985 Miners' strike takes place.

1987 Work begins on the Cardiff Bay Development.

1996 Welsh regions are replaced by 22 unitary authorities.

1997 Wales votes in favour of a Welsh Assembly.

1999 Millennium Stadium, now Principality Stadium, opened in Cardiff.

2005 BBC broadcasts first *Doctor Who* episodes made in Cardiff.

2008 Last deep coalmine in Wales closes.

2012 The Welsh and English languages are given equal status in the Senedd for the first time, when The National Assembly for Wales (Official Languages) Act 2012 receives royal assent.

2018 The Second Severn Crossing is renamed the 'Prince of Wales Bridge'.

2022 Upon the death of Queen Elizabeth II, William, the elder son of newly crowned King Charles III, is confirmed as the new Prince of Wales while his wife Catherine becomes Princess of Wales.

Index

A
abbeys 80
Abercarn 134
Aberfan 159
Abergavenny 42, 104
Aberystwyth 106, 142
Abraham, William 'Mabon' 146
Ambrosius Aurelianus 55, 56
Anarawd 73, 75
Angles 59, 60
Anglesey (Môn) 43, 70, 75
Arthur 56, 57, 58, 59

B
Beaumaris 106, 177
Bersham 7, 8, 126, 127
Blaenafon 152
Blaenau Ffestiniog 129, 131
Bleddyn ap Cynfyn 86
Blue Books 145
Boudicca (Boadicea) 43
Boyce, Max 163
Brycheiniog (Brecon) 63, 74, 76, 78, 87, 89, 104
Brynmawr 132, 151
Buellt 74, 76, 78, 87

C
Cadwallon ap Cadfan 14
Caerleon 42, 43, 44, 52
Caernarfon 42, 103, 106, 128, 177
Caerwent 45
Caerwys 21, 106
Caractacus 39, 40
Cardiff 17, 42, 51, 104, 143, 161, 173, 179
Carew 7, 104
Carmarthen 8, 42, 45, 93, 109
Carreg Cennen 104
cattle 19, 29, 49, 79, 110, 126
Celtic gods 38
Celts 10, 31, 32, 34, 35, 36, 44, 48, 49
Centre for Alternative Technology 174-5
Ceredigion (Cardigan) 21, 25, 63, 74, 88
Charles II 124
Charles, Prince of Wales 154, 155
Chepstow 65
Chester 8, 62, 66
Chirk 127
Church, Charlotte 166
circulating schools 125
coalmining 8, 126, 132, 133, 140-141, 147, 150, 151, 156, 162
Coity 104
Conwy 70, 106, 114, 177
Cornovii 35
Cornwall 30, 66, 67
Corwen 21
Criccieth 106
Crug Mawr, Battle of 88
Cumbria 66, 67
Cunedda 25, 50
Cwmcarn 19
Cymry 12, 53, 63
Cynddylan 66

Wales A Very Peculiar History

D

daffodils 121
Dafydd ap Gwilym 108
Dafydd ap Llywelyn 95
David, St 25, 80, 165
Deceangli 35, 43
Deganwy 61
Deheubarth 21, 63, 76, 83, 87, 88
Demetae 35
Dinas Emrys 8, 55
Doctor Who 173
druids 37, 43
Dyfed 63, 74, 76

E

Ebbw Vale 138
Edward I 98, 101, 103
Edward III 107
Edward VIII 151, 152, 154
eisteddfodau 8, 14, 21, 136, 137, 145
Eryri 18, 83, 176

F

farming 29, 48, 126
Felinfoel 6
Ffestiniog Railway 131
Flint 106

G

Gelert 99
George V 154
Gildas, St 24, 60
Glamorgan *see* Morgannwg
Glaslyn, River 55

Glyndŵr, Owain 111, 112
Glywysing 63, 80
gold mining 31, 45, 178
Gower 13, 16
Gruffydd ap Cynan 87, 88, 94
Gruffydd ap Elisedd 69
Gruffydd ap Llywelyn 8, 81, 83
Gruffydd of Gwent 69
gwely 71, 72, 77
Gwenllian 94
Gwent 63, 69, 87
Gwernvale 8
Gwynedd 8, 55, 61, 63, 73, 75, 76, 78, 86, 87, 88, 95, 98, 101, 102, 103

H

Harlech 8, 106, 122, 123, 177
Harold II 83, 84
harps 120
Hay-on-Wye 160
Hendy-gwyn 77
Hengist 54
Henry III 95
Henry IV 111
Henry V 8, 112
Henry VII 113
Henry VIII 113, 115, 118
'Hen Wlad fy Nhadau' 137
Hereford 82
Holywell 127, 128
Honorius 50, 52
Hywel Dda (the Good) 76, 77, 78, 79, 102, 108

Index

I
Idwal ap Anarawd 76

J
Jenkins, Katherine 166
Jones, Thomas 21

K
Kidwelly 94

L
'Land of My Fathers' 137
Laws in Wales Acts 10, 113, 116, 117
leeks 6, 14, 121, 163
Llandudno 8
Llanelli 6, 132
Llanerchaeron 19
Llanfairpwllgwyngyll-gogerychwyrndrobwll-llantysiliogogogoch 7
Llangollen 130
Llantwit Major 48, 80
Llanwrtyd Wells 19
Lleyn Peninsula 52, 70
Llyn Cerrig Bach 33
Llyn Fawr 32
Lloyd George, David 148, 149, 150
Llwynon 13
Llywarch ap Hyfaidd 76
Llywelyn ap Seisyll 78, 79
Llywelyn Bren 107
Llywelyn the Great 95
Llywelyn the Last 8, 96, 98, 99, 101
Lostprophets 17
love spoons 121

M
Mabinogion 92, 97
Madoc 91
Madog ap Llywelyn 107
Maelgwn 61, 80
Maesteg 132
Manic Street Preachers 17
Maredudd ap Owain 78
'Marwnad Cynddylan' 66
Menai Strait 6
Merfyn 73
Merlin 58
Merthyr Tydfil 126, 142
Methodism 123, 125
Meurig ap Hywel 69
Milford Haven 113
Millennium Centre 17
Millennium Stadium 166
Mold 127
monasteries 80
Monmouthshire 10
Mordred 59
Morgan, William 119
Morgannwg 74, 83, 86, 87, 88
Morganwg, Iolo 8, 136
Mudiad Amddiffyn Cymru 159

N
National Museum 17
national parks 18
Neath 18, 42, 126, 138
Newborough 106
Newport 144
Noncomformists 14, 123, 124, 125, 145–146, 148
Normans 84–88

Wales A Very Peculiar History

O
Offa 10, 64, 65
Ordovicii 35, 43
Ostorius Scapula 43

P
Parry, Bishop 119
Paulinus, Gaius Suetonius 43
Pembroke 70, 104
Penal Code 112
Penrhyn 128, 130
Plaid Cymru 8, 157, 158, 161, 164
Pontnewydd 8
Pontypool 6, 126, 132
Portmeirion 150
Powys 64, 73, 78, 80, 81, 87, 101
Prestatyn 65

R
Rebecca Riots 144
recipes 22-23, 79
Rhodri Mawr 73, 74, 75
Rhondda 13, 134, 138
Rhuddlan 106
 Statute of 101-102
Rhys ap Gruffydd 21
Romans 8, 10, 36, 37, 39-52, 66
rugby 6, 20, 166

S
St David's Day 19
Seisyllwg 73, 74, 76
Senghenydd 134
Severn, River 64, 66, 70
sheep 29, 49
Silures 35, 43
slate 7, 128, 129
Snowdonia (Eryri) 18, 83, 176
Super Furry Animals 17
Swansea 7, 126

T
Taff 138, 143
Taliesin 74
Torchwood 173
tourism 16-19, 176, 177
Tryweryn Valley 157

U
Usk 42, 43
Uther 56

V
Vikings 74, 78
Vortigern 53, 54, 56

W
Wales, arms of 100
Welsh Assembly 8, 10, 162, 164
Welsh flag 15, 165
Welsh language 10, 14, 21, 66, 105, 116, 117, 129, 139, 148, 152-153, 158, 168-170, 172, 180-181
Welsh Parliament 112
White Castle 104
Wilkinson, John 7, 127
Wrexham 7, 134
Wroxeter 43